107 BEST WALKS

By Allan C. Kimball

The Great Texas Line Press
Fort Worth, Texas

Dedicated to my buddy George who accompanied me on many of these walks, and to my wife Madonna who went along on several walks and who accompanies me on the walk of life.

Cover photo by Allan C. Kimball
Back cover photos by Laurence Parent, Allan C. Kimball and George Colvin
Cover design: Kari Crane

Contents

East Texas

Gulf Coast

Hill Country and Central Texas

South Texas

West Texas

Introduction

This book serves as a guide to some of the best places in Texas where you can get out and walk. Says who? Says me, a self-appointed expert who acknowledges that these aren't the only places to walk in a place as sprawling as Texas, and some walks aren't for everyone.

Even selecting 107 places is simply an arbitrary number. But they are a good place to start. To be included, a walk had to be interesting in some way, and that it not be too long or too difficult.

The walks are divided up by geographical regions in Texas. And each is listed with details explaining what makes it special, its length, its location, and contact information. Some are more like hikes.

The Lost Mine Peak Trail in Big Bend National Park is a moderately strenuous walk up a clear path that begins at about a mile high and goes up for another couple thousand feet. It's not for those who are completely out of shape. But if you walk regularly it should be no problem since much of the path consists of switchbacks. Just go at a comfortable pace. The rewards are phenomenal. First, you have the walk itself, passing through thick forest and then passing by cactus and ocotillo and agave. Second is the panoramic view at the top that will take your breath away if the walk itself hasn't already done that.

Some walks are literally walks in the park, along paths built by cities expressly for the purpose of strolling. Some are in commercial establishments. Mall walking got to be popular in the 1990s and remains so. What's not to like? You get to stroll around in air-conditioned comfort and can top your walk off with a refreshment, maybe even buy a birthday present somewhere along the way. By walking around The Ballpark in Arlington, home of the Texas Rangers baseball club, you can be amazed at all the architectural details in its construction as you amble around and learn about star players featured on its Wall of Fame.

Some of these walks will take you into the depths of the earth. Longhorn Cavern near Burnet is a unique cave formed by flowing water so it doesn't have many of the usual cave formations. Sauntering down there is like roaming inside a smooth marble vault. On summer weekends, you can be entertained by musicians really getting down.

We are made to walk. We walk upright on two legs—we don't runeverywhere we go, we don't amble about on four legs like most mammals,and we don't use our knuckles on the ground for balance like other primates. We may spend the majority of our work day bound to a desk, a majority of our leisure time surfing the Internet, and a significant amount of all our time texting or tweeting. We may pull our weight, climb every mountain, or paddle our own canoe. We might even pedal/swim/run a triathlon every now and then. But none of that is what we're made for.

We are made to walk.

Allan C. Kimball
Wimberley, Texas

East Texas

Atlanta—Atlanta State Park

Trail: Arrowhead Trail
Length: 1 mile/moderate
Location: 11 miles northwest of Atlanta off Farm Road 1154.
Information: 927 Park Road 42, Atlanta, TX 75551, 903-796-6476, tpwd.texas.gov/state-parks/atlanta
Best Time to Visit: Anytime, but winter mornings may be cold.
Why Go: Walk through the pine forest where the Caddo Indians once walked. Like many of the East Texas walks, this one meanders around thick stands of tall pines. Because this trail is almost exclusively within the forest, it is always shaded so the walk isn't too bad in the summer. The trail is a wide dirt trail cushioned so thickly by pine needles in some places that walking on it is like walking on a feather bed: easy on the feet. If you go in the spring, you'll discover lots of dogwood blooms. If you head out early in the morning, you'll share the path with lots of wildlife. About midway along the trail is an overlook of Lake Wright Patman, the main reason most people visit the park.

Atlanta State Park.
Photo by Allan C. Kimball

Crockett—Davy Crockett National Forest

Trail: Four C National Recreation Trail
Length: As long as 20 miles/easy
Location: Off Texas 7, 15 miles east of Crockett.
Information: Davy Crockett National Forest, 18551 Texas 7 East, Kennard, TX 75847, 936-655-2299, http://www.fs.usda.gov/texas/
Best Time to Visit: Anytime, but be careful in November and December when deer hunters are lurking in the forest.
Why Go: This 20-mile-long trail begins at Ratcliff Lake and winds through a diverse forest of towering pines, bottomland hardwoods, boggy sloughs, and upland forests. Midway down the trail is the Walnut Creek campsite with five tent pads, a shelter, and a pit toilet. The

walk wanders through pine forests, bottomland hardwoods, boggy sloughs, and upland forests. Start your trek either at Ratcliff Lake and go as far as you please, then return, or go the entire 20 miles. Or you can do the same at the north end of the trail, taking in the Neches Bluff Overlook that offers a panoramic view of pine-hardwood forests in the Neches River bottomlands. The trail follows abandoned tramways built by the Central Coal and Coke Company that once logged timber in the area; it's marked with white rectangular tags and is easy to follow.

Daingerfield—Daingerfield State Park

Trail: Hiking Trail
Length: 2.5 miles/strenuous
Location: 2 miles east of Daingerfield off Texas 49.
Information: 455 Park Road 17, Daingerfield, TX 75638, 903-645-2921, tpwd.texas.gov/state-parks/daingerfield
Best Time to Visit: Avoid summers.
Why Go: Go into the real heart of a pine forest while being serenaded by birds and cicadas the entire way. The dirt trail is cushioned with pine needles but it is crossed with so many narrow roots in places that you have to be very careful to make certain you don't trip. Also, many visitors have created their own paths through the woods, so make certain you're on the right trail—you can tell because the trees are marked with small "AVA" metal signs because the American Volkssport Association holds regular walks here. This trail climbs a steep hill and is so isolated among the towering pines that if you have a tendency toward claustrophobia, don't go. One portion near the end is exceptionally steep, so, again, watch your steps. Go in the spring to see all the dogwood and redbud trees blooming alongside wisteria vines. And the fall colors, as the sweetgum and maples trees turn bright red, aren't bad, either.

*Daingerfield State Park.
Photo by Allan C. Kimball*

Fairfield—Fairfield Lake State Park

Trail: Nature Trail
Length: 2-mile loop/easy
Location: 6 miles northeast of Fairfield off Farm Road 3285.
Information: 123 State Park Road 64, Fairfield, TX 75840, 903-389-4514, tpwd.texas.gov/state-parks/fairfield-lake
Best Time to Visit: Anytime.
Why Go: This is a very relaxing trail. It's another walk through the woods, this time through a post oak savannah and blue stem grasses, a transition topography from the piney woods of the east to the prairie grasslands to the north and west. The trail is a wide, dirt path almost always in full shade. Because the trail loops out over a peninsula, Fairfield Lake is always visible, and the sound of boats on the lake are the only thing to disrupt the chirping of birds and peck-peck-peck of the wood-peckers you'll almost always come across. Sometimes you'll even hear an obnoxious duck along the trail. Along the path are two lake over-looks, and a picnic table is located about midway. Take your time at the first overlook, where you might see an osprey diving into the water for lunch. If you're an angler, bring your favorite pole because the fishing is excellent, even in winter because the adjacent power plant uses lake water to cool the facility, discharging warm water.

Huntsville—Huntsville State Park

Trail: Dogwood Trail
Length: 1.75 miles/moderate
Location: 6 miles southwest of Huntsville off Interstate 45.
Information: P.O. Box 508, Huntsville, TX 77342, 936-295-5644, tpwd.texas.gov/state-parks/huntsville
Best Time to Visit: Anytime, but the dogwood blooms are special in the spring.
Why Go: Begin at the park's Nature Center. This is a nice loop walk, with enough ups and downs to keep things interesting. You stroll through the piney woods—loblolly and shortleaf pine trees tower above you, plus enough dogwood trees to provide variety and extra beauty when they break out in delicate white blooms. The trail is well-marked and well-maintained, but you need to watch for exposed tree roots that will catch your feet if

you're not careful. The trail is also heavily traveled because it is close to prime camping areas around Lake Raven, so you will have company. Because the trail is close to the lake and creeks, you're also likely to spy lots of wildlife if you're out and about in the morning. Deer, birds, opossums, and lots of armadillos are seen along the trail. And you might spy snakes in the woods and alligators in the lake.

Jasper—Angelina National Forest

Trail: Sawmill
Length: 5.5 miles/easy
Location: Along the north and south shores of Lake Sam Rayburn near Jasper, on Forest Service Road 313.
Information: 111 Walnut Ridge Road, Zavalla, TX 75980, 936-897-1068, http://www.fs.usda.gov/texas
Best Time to Visit: Anytime, but summers can be hot and humid
Why Go: Most non-Texans picture the state being all cactus and desert, but the piney woods of East Texas prove that stereotype dead wrong and nowhere more so than Angelina National Forest. The trail goes over gently rolling terrain and winds through the pine forest between Bouton Lake and Boykin Springs Lake recreation areas. In addition to the shaded natural beauty all around, the trail has a fair amount of history to it—a portion follows an old tramway used to haul logs to sawmills and one section of the trail leads to the Aldridge Sawmill ruins. Get a map of the trail at the ranger's office or at the trailhead at Boykin Springs where you'll also find restrooms, showers and drinking water. By the way, that knocking sound you seem to be hearing constantly is one of several woodpeckers that call this forest home. One of them, the red-cockaded woodpecker, is endangered and quite rare.

Jasper—Martin Dies Jr. State Park

Trail: Slough Trail
Length: 2.2 miles/easy
Location: 12 miles west of Jasper off U.S. 190.
Information: 634 Private Road 5025, Jasper, TX 75951, 409-384-5231 tpwd.texas.gov/state-parks/martin-dies-jr
Best Time to Visit: Anytime but summer.

Why Go: At the edge of the Big Thicket National Preserve, you'll find numerous creeks and a forest markedly different from the pines of much of East Texas. Here are beech, cypress, magnolia, and willow trees, and in the fall the gold of the beech leaves stand out. Look up a lot—you're likely to see a bald eagle or two in winter. The Slough Trail is also quite different from the Big Thicket because it meanders around a swamp area at the end of Gum Slough, a tributary of B.A. Steinhagen Reservoir. It's here that you're likely to see the most birds. After several recent hurricanes, you're also likely to see lots of downed trees and various fungi clinging to tree trunks. Because this is not a loop, you should add another half-mile to the distance to get back to your car. And because of all the damage caused by hurricanes, before you head out to the park call the headquarters to make certain which portions are open.

Kountze—Big Thicket National Preserve

Trail: Sundew Trail
Length: 1.6-mile outer loop/easy
Location: In the Hickory Creek Savannah Unit, 4.2 miles south of Warren on Farm Road 2827 off U.S. 69/287.
Information: 6044 Farm Road 420, Kountze, TX 77625, 409-951-6725, www.nps.gov/bith
Best Time to Visit: Spring for wildflowers. Summers are hot and humid. Closed on government holidays.
Why Go: This place is called "big thicket" for a good reason: The brush and woods are so thick that even the local Native Americans stayed out except for occasional hunting and settlers didn't venture into the area until near the end of the 19th century. Even today you won't find many people, just lots and lots of forest. This is a top wildflower viewing area and even when the flowers aren't in bloom you can spot pitcher plants and sundew— both carnivorous. The trail also has an inner loop of just less than a mile that is mostly boardwalk. Might as well do both loops.

Big Thicket National Preserve. National Park Service Photo

Livingston—Lake Livingston State Park

Trail: Pineywoods Nature Walk

Length: 1 mile loop/easy

Location: 1 mile southwest of Livingston off U.S. 59.

Information: 300 Park Road 65, Livingston, TX 77351, 936-365-2201, tpwd.texas.gov/state-parks/lake-livingston

Best Time to Visit: Anytime.

Why Go: This is a boardwalk loop through the forest and by the wetlands, past a duck pond, a frog pond, and a hummingbird garden. The forest you're walking through is mostly loblolly pine and water oak. The trail has an observation deck and rest area, along with a picnic area and interpretive signs by the frog pond. If you are observant, you will see white-tail deer in the distance. Squirrels and swamp rabbits are common, too, along

Lake Livingston State Park.
Photo by Allan C. Kimball

with egrets at the duck pond (in fact, you're more likely to see egrets and herons than ducks). The trail is also handicapped accessible. If you plan on camping here, bear in mind that this park is extremely popular with people from the Houston area and campsites go quickly on weekends. If you're here for the walking, don't worry because most of the crowd is here for lake recreation.

Lufkin—Azalea Trail

Length: 4 miles round trip/easy

Location: Richardson Park is at Loop 287 and Mott Drive, Kiwanis Park is at Timberland and South First streets.

Information: City of Lufkin Parks and Recreation, P.O. Drawer 190, Lufkin, TX 75904-0190, 936-633-0250, www.lufkinparks.com

Best Time to Visit: Anytime, dawn to dusk.

Why Go: The Azalea Trail is surrounded by shopping malls and restaurants and is one of the most popular walking trails in the city. As the path begins, it is lined with several azalea bushes, and then drops into a variety of lush vegetation. The trail follows Hurricane Creek, a hardwood wetlands, connecting Grace Dunne Richardson Park and Kiwanis

Park and the woods are so thick that often you don't hear the sounds of all the traffic. You also won't see any traffic except when the trail runs by a mall parking lot. You cross major streets by going under and through drainage structures. The trail is mostly pine bark and sand. The trail is lit by many lamplights and many of the poles are tagged with mileage markers. You'll also find benches and call boxes. Restrooms and showers are at Richardson Park. By the way, don't confuse this walking Azalea Trail in Lufkin with the driving Azalea Trail event held each spring in nearby Tyler.

Lufkin—Ellen Trout Park and Zoo

Length: 1.5 miles/easy
Location: On Loop 287 in Lufkin, off Martin Luther King Street.
Information: 402 Zoo Circle, Lufkin, TX 75904, 936-633-0399, www.ellentroutzoo.com
Best Time to Visit: Open 9 a.m. to 5 p.m. daily.
Why Go: Walk through the wildest place in town, home to more than 800 birds, mammals, and reptiles from around the world. The walkway wanders through nicely landscaped and shaded areas, almost in a maze. Strollers will be joined by many peacocks and peahens roaming free. If you're lucky, you might see a peacock displaying his amazing tail fan of feathers for one of his hen friends. Most of the animals here are in cages or glass enclosures. A small zoo, Ellen Trout is interesting for some of the more unusual animals such as the Malayan tapir, endangered Siamese crocodile, the clouded leopard, and the Maasai giraffe. You'll find a play-ground and picnic area near the entrance, overlooking Ellen Trout Lake. Restrooms, benches and picnic areas are located at various places inside the zoo. After your walk, relax on the Z&OO Railroad, which will take you around the zoo and across the lake.

Ellen Park Zoo Tiger. Photo by Allan C. Kimball

Lumberton—Village Creek State Park

Trail: Tupelo Trail and Village Creek Trail
Length: 2 miles/easy
Location: 10 miles north of Beaumont, off U.S. 69 on Farm Road 3513.
Information: P.O. Box 8565, Lumberton, TX 77657, 409-755-7322, tpwd.texas.gov/state-parks/village-creek
Best Time to Visit: Avoid summers
Why Go: Combining these two trails lets you experience Village Creek, an extremely popular canoeing stream, and the Tupelo Swamp. Once, you would be surrounded by all sorts of impres-

Village Creek State Park.
© Earl Nottingham, TPWD

sive trees along the dirt trail, from cypress to yaupon, but many of those trees were lost in Hurricane Ike in 2008. It'll take awhile for them to come back. But still, the park has a wide variety of plant and animal species rarely found in the same place anywhere on earth. More than 1,000 types of plants, more than 100 trees, more than 200 bird species and just about any animal you can think of. Walking here is like going back in time into a cypress swamp with snakes slithering here and there and carnivorous plants snapping shut on insect breakfasts.

New Waverly—Sam Houston National Forest's Double Lake Recreation Area

Trail: Lakeside Trail
Length: 8 miles/easy
Location: On Farm Road 2025, off Texas 150, 25 miles east of New Waverly.
Information: 394 Farm Road 1375 West, New Waverly, TX 77358, 936-344-6205 or 888-361-6908, www.fs.fed.us/r8/texas
Best Time to Visit: Anytime.
Why Go: The relatively flat trail circles the 24-acre lake, but eight miles is a pretty long walk, so just tackle the distance you feel up for that day. The easy-to- follow hard-packed trail goes by whispering pines and hardwoods that keep you shaded. The woods are so thick in some areas that you'll think that you're walking through a tall, leafy tunnel. And if you've worked up a sweat, just jump in the lake.

Phelps—Sam Houston National Forest

Trail: Lone Star Hiking Trail's Four Notch Loop

Length: 9 miles/moderate

Location: Off Forest Service 213, off Four Notch Road from Farm Road 2296, about 7 miles southeast of Phelps.

Information: Sam Houston National Forest, 394 Farm Road 1375 West, New Waverly, TX 77358, 936-344-6205, www.fs.fed.us/r8/texas

Best Time to Visit: Late fall through spring; summers can be unbearable.

Why Go: Start early: This is a long walk. The trailhead and parking lot are at Forest Service Road 213. Check with forest headquarters to get a map and instructions on how to access the trail. The trail, which is marked with aluminum rectangles and easy to follow, is a loop through the forest. The first portion is relatively open, but then enters the woods where the tall pines keep you shaded. You'll go up and down through lowlands crowded with palmettos and ferns and cross a couple of creeks. You'll cross Boswell Creek twice and it can be difficult to cross if it's rained heavily. At peak times, you'll likely see other walkers and maybe several campers, but for the most part you will have the trail to yourself. During deer hunting season in November and December, you should probably wear very bright, highly visible clothing. And use lots of insect repellent between late spring and early fall.

Tyler—Municipal Rose Gardens

Tyler Municipal Rose Gardens.
Photo by Allan C. Kimball

Trail: Rose Garden and Rose Museum

Length: 2 miles/easy

Location: Texas 31 at Rose Park Drive.

Information: 420 Rose Park Drive, Tyler, TX 75702, 903-597-3130, www.texasrosefestival.com/museum/garden.htm

Best Time to Visit: Anytime, but spring is best for all the blooming flowers.

Why Go: This paved walkway through flowering gardens of mostly roses—all sorts and sizes and types—is a relaxing and inspiring place to spend a little time. How many roses?

How about 38,000 bushes displaying 500 varieties. The 14-acre garden is the largest municipal rose garden in the U.S. In many areas, the fragrant path is shaded by tall pines and oaks, and in one section goes around a fountain that constantly varies its spurting designs. Along the way, you'll also find a large koi pond, a gazebo, a meditation garden, and an idea garden. All the various flowering plants are labeled. Adjacent to the garden is the Rose Museum, which has a history of roses, a history of the city's huge Rose Festival (every October), and Tyler historical artifacts. Among the features of the museum are the displays of the impressive Rose Queen gowns—so impressive that you will find it difficult not to say "Wow!"

Tyler—Tyler State Park

Trail: Lakeside Trail
Length: 2.5 miles/moderate
Location: 2 miles north of Interstate 20 in Tyler off Farm Road 14.
Information: 789 Park Road 16, Tyler, TX 75706-9141, 903-597-5338, tpwd.texas.gov/state-parks/tyler
Best Time to Visit: Anytime.
Why Go: This is one fine walk, my favorite in East Texas. It would be tempting to call this just another walk through the woods—and it is—but it's a perfect walk through the woods. The path is smooth, the trees surround it, and you will feel like a part of nature. It is always interesting. The trail is mostly a dirt trail through the

Tyler State Park. Photo by Allan C. Kimball

piney woods encircling the park's lake, with boardwalks over some marshy areas. The vegetation and shade are much thicker on the western portion of the walk because the eastern end follows the lake's beach area. You'll find benches and picnic tables on the trail, with one particular bench under the pines overlooking the lake at a strategic point on the south end that will offer great views of the sunset. The trail is moderately hilly, but nothing strenuous. A small portion of the trail follows the park road, so be careful there, just stay close to the lake shore. Maple, ash, and birch trees turn crimson in the fall.

GULF COAST

Austwell—Aransas National Wildlife Refuge

Trail: Dagger Point Trail and Alligator Viewing Area
Length: Dagger Point 1 mile/easy, Alligator one-tenth of a mile/easy.
Location: About 7 miles south of Austwell on Farm Road 2040.
Information: P.O. Box 100, Austwell, TX 77950, 361-286-3559, www.fws.gov/refuge/aransas/

Best Time to Visit: Late fall through early spring to see rare whooping cranes.

Why Go: The refuge is the vacation home to the largest flock of wintering whooping cranes in North America, about 200 birds. The whoopers are big birds about 5 feet high with a wingspan averaging 7 feet. They once approached extinction. Don't settle for the rare birds, though—head on over to the

Rare whooping cranes at Aransas National Wildlife Refuge. © Earl Nottingham, TPWD

Alligator Viewing Area where gators come out to bask on the banks. The 115,000-acre saltmarsh and coastal prairie refuge complex has several short trails and, if you feel up to it, you can do all of them easily in a day. Along the trails you'll find observation platforms, telescopes, a photo blind, and panoramic vistas. One of the few hills in the refuge is along this trail, giving you a great view of the bay. Mottes—islands of trees—dot the refuge. Don't just scoot by them, slow down and pay attention because mottes of oak and redbay trees are prime hiding places for deer, javelina, and bobcats. Bring mosquito repellent.

Brazoria—San Bernard National Wildlife Refuge

Trail: Bobcat Woods Trail
Length: 1.75 miles/easy
Location: About 10 miles southwest of Lake Jackson, off Farm Road 2918.
Information: 6801 County Road 306, Brazoria, TX 77422, 979-964-3639, www.fws.gov/refuge/san_bernard/
Best Time to Visit: Avoid late spring and summers.

Why Go: This is essentially a birding trail that wanders along the edge of a marsh through occasionally thick woods. The trail is mostly a boardwalk, but you will also discover a few dirt paths that go for short distances from the main trail. You'll find a number of benches and an observation platform, where you can sit quietly and listen to the songbirds or watch for all sorts of neo-tropical birds that make the refuge their home or fly through during migrations—everything from bald eagles to sandpipers, perhaps even a rare whooping crane. The trail has many interpretive signs, giving you all sorts of information on habitats or birds or

San Bernard National Wildlife Refuge.
Photo by Allan C. Kimball

mosquitoes. About those mosquitoes: They can be so thick at certain times of the year they can drive a walker insane. So if you do go in late spring or the summer, bring industrial strength bug repellent and slather it on. Even that may not be enough. Restrooms are in the parking area.

Corpus Christi—Padre Island National Seashore

Trail: Malaquite Beach
Length: About 4 miles roundtrip/easy
Location: 13 miles south of Corpus Christi on Park Road 22 along North Padre Island.
Information: P.O. Box 181300, Corpus Christi, TX 78480, 361-949-8068, www.nps.gov/pais
Best Time to Visit: Anytime.
Why Go: This is not actually a trail, just a walk on the beach. The park service allows vehicles on much of North Padre Island, but this section, from the barricade at North Beach to the barricade at South Beach, allows you to walk in the pristine sand without having to dodge pickups or four-wheelers. Well, sometimes a park staff member will zip by on a four-wheeler but that's all. Take in the fresh sea breeze, check the sand for seashells and sea beans, and watch overhead for flocks of pelicans. While the park allows you to collect any shells or driftwood you find, be careful because hazardous Portuguese Man o' War frequently wash up on the shore, too. You'll find parking lots at North Beach, South Beach,

and at the Malaquite Visitors Center, just behind the dunes. The Visitors Center has a small museum, gift shop, restrooms and showers. In the same area, on the beach, are several shaded picnic tables. One unusual amenity on Padre Island is that the National Park Service has one wheelchair designed for use on loose sand that is available for loan at no charge. Call ahead.

Corpus Christi's Malaquite Beach at Padre Island National Seashore. Photo by Allan C. Kimball

Corpus Christi—Seawall

Length: 1.75 miles one-way/easy

Location: From the Convention Center to Buford Street, along Shoreline Boulevard.

Information: 1823 N. Chaparral St., Corpus Christi, TX 78401, 800-766-2322, www.corpuschristivb.com

Best Time to Visit: Anytime.

Why Go: The seawall is essentially on the Gulf of Mexico side of the entire length of Shoreline Boulevard. The steps of the 14-foot-high seawall look like a stairway into the Gulf. Along the seawall are a marina, hotels, offices, and the Selena Memorial. Unique aspects of the Corpus Christi Seawall are the Miradores de Mary bay-front gazebos, replicas of similar structures in Morocco and Spain. Unlike the Galveston Seawall, you won't be distracted by many shops and restaurants along the way—what you'll see on the mainland side are hotels and office buildings and a couple restaurants, while on the Gulf side you'll see marinas, waves and birds. The seawall is also near such attractions as the Art Center, the USS Lexington, the Texas State Aquarium, and the replicas of Christopher Columbus' ships.

Corpus Christi Seawall. Photo by Allan C. Kimball

Galveston—Seawall

Length: 7 miles one-way/easy

Location: From East Beach to Magic Carpet Miniature Golf along Seawall Boulevard.

Information: Galveston Island Visitors Center, 2067 61st St., Galveston, TX 77551, 888-425-4753, www.galveston.com

Best Time to Visit: Anytime.

Galveston's seawall. Photo by Allan C. Kimball

Why Go: Taking a walk along the Galveston Seawall is one of the most relaxing yet invigorating walks you can take in all of Texas, thanks to the sea breezes and salt air and sounds of the surf from the Gulf of Mexico just a stone's throw away. The seawall was built in 1910, ten years after the Great Storm of 1900 devastated a third of the city, killing more than 6,000 people and ending Galveston's prominent place among Texas cities. The wall is 7 miles long and 17 feet high, a protective barrier for the city against the surging fury of another hurricane. It runs for 54,790 feet, about a third of the island's Gulf frontage. On the opposite side of the street, you'll discover all sorts of gift shops, restaurants, motels, and snack shops. You can access the beach from several locations along the seawall, so you can either take a refreshing dip during your walk, or walk all or parts of it in the sand. The beach side was restored after Hurricane Ike in 2008.

Galveston—The Strand

Length: 2 miles/easy

Location: North of downtown Galveston along Strand and adjacent streets.

Information: Galveston Island Visitors Center, 2328 Broadway, Galveston, TX 77550, 888-425-4753, www.galveston.com

Best Time to Visit: Anytime.

Why Go: You can make this walk as long or as short as you'd like just by varying the number of city blocks you walk. For the best route, begin at 25th and Strand streets, wander toward the Gulf along Harborside Street, out onto the piers, down to 20th Street. Then walk up to Ship Mechanics Row, and back toward 25th. The sidewalk will take you to a number of

Sailing ship Elissa is docked next to modern cruise ship on Galveston's Strand. Photo by Allan C. Kimball.

restaurants and shops featuring everything from surf-and-sun goodies and souvenirs to antiques, all housed in historic buildings. Along the walk you also have the chance to visit the Galveston Island Railroad Museum, the Ocean Star Offshore Energy Center and Museum at Pier 19, the Pier 21 Theater featuring the *Great Storm* and the *Pirate Island of Jean Lafite* films, the Texas Seaport Museum with the tall ship *Elissa*, and the renowned Colonel Bubbie's—billed as the world's only authentic military surplus store. You should visit each of these, which will add more mileage to your walk.

Houston—Arboretum

Trail: Alice Brown Trail and Inner Loop Trail
Length: 1 mile/easy
Location: At Loop 610 and Woodway.
Information: 4501 Woodway Drive, Houston, TX 770248, 713-681-8433, www.houstonarboretum.org
Best Time to Visit: 7 a.m. to 7 p.m. daily.
Why Go: These two loops make for an interesting walk right in the heart of the city, where the sounds of nature compete with the sounds of traffic. The arboretum is a 155-acre preserve in Memorial Park and is home to more than 75 varieties of native trees, 160 species of birds, and

Houston Arboretum. Photo by Allan C. Kimball

33 kinds of butterflies. Lots of turtles and frogs, too. The trail is a dirt path along a boardwalk through thick brush and by several tall trees. The dirt portion of the trail is covered with bark mulch making it very comfortable to walk on. The Nature Center not only has a gift shop and nature exhibits, but also hosts several educational programs during the year, where you can learn such things as how fast dragonflies zoom past and which turtles breathe through their butts.

Houston—Discovery Green

Length: 1.5 miles/easy
Location: Between McKinney and Lamar streets in downtown Houston, across from the George R. Brown Convention Center.
Information: Discovery Green Conservancy, 1500 McKinney St., Houston, TX 77010, 713-400-7336, www.discoverygreen.com
Best Time to Visit: Hours vary.

Houston's Discovery Green. Photo by Allan C. Kimball

Why Go: Opened in 2008, this is a walk around and through a 12-acre urban park in downtown Houston near the convention center and Minute Maid Park where the Houston Astros play ball. The walkway is a paved sidewalk that circles the park and bisects it. The park is nicely landscaped but this isn't the place to come to commune with nature because of all the commuter traffic surrounding you and the children frolicking in one of the park's two fountains or in the playground. The walkway has lots of benches in shaded rest areas under oak and cypress trees. You'll also find some nice sculptures. The park also regularly hosts special events and regular exercise programs.

Houston—Galleria

Length: 2.5 miles/easy
Location: At the intersection of Westheimer Road and Post Oak Boulevard off Loop 610.
Information: 5085 Westheimer Road, Suite 4850, Houston, TX 77056, 713-622-0663, www.galleriahouston.com
Best Time to Visit: 10 a.m. to 9 p.m. Monday through Saturday, 11 a.m. to 7 p.m. Sunday.
Why Go: With 3 million square feet and more than 375 stores, you can mall walk in the largest indoor shopping center in Texas and the fourth largest in the U.S. Like the

*Houston's Galleria Mall.
Photo by Allan C. Kimball*

sprawling metropolis of Houston, the Galleria is pleasantly excessive. The mall features stunning architecture highlighted by several types of stone and wood, suspended glass balconies, and stores set below spectacular glass atriums. Along the mall's three main floors, you'll find restaurants from steaks to seafood, two hotels, lots of snack areas, and lots of stuff to buy including one store that specializes in walking shoes. It's almost too many options. Opened in 1970, the mall has been expanded several times so that now it has four arms. Oh, and there's an ice skating rink if you want still more exercise.

Houston—Memorial Park

Trail: Seymour Lieberman Exercise Trail
Length: 3 miles/easy
Location: Near I-10 and I-610 West Loop.
Information: 6501 Memorial Drive, Houston, TX 77007, 713-865-4500, www.houstontx.gov/parks/memorialpark.html
Best Time to Visit: Anytime, dawn to dusk (but avoid midday hours during the summer because of heat).
Why Go: This is where a large number of Houston's fitness aficionados go when they want some exercise. The park, in the heart of the city but away from crowded downtown, is a 1,500-acre lush oasis among the concrete. The trail is crushed granite and packed earth, much easier on your feet than the pavement some cities use in their park trails. If you want to do more than just stroll, exercise stations are located along the trail with a workout station near the tennis center. The trail is lighted and has restrooms and water fountains. The park also has a golf course, tennis courts, biking trails, a fitness center, croquet courts, a swimming pool, and picnic areas. Larger than New York's Central Park, this is the best city park in the state.

Houston—Zoo

Length: 2.5 miles/easy
Location: In Herman Park at 6200 Golf Course Drive in downtown Houston.
Information: 1513 N. MacGregor Dr., Houston, TX 77030, 713-533-6500, www.houstonzoo.org

Best Time to Visit: Nov. 2 to March 7, 9 a.m. to 6 p.m. March 8 to Nov. 1, 9 a.m. to 7 p.m.. Closed Christmas.

Why Go: This is a truly top notch zoo, and every Houstonian knows it, making it one of the most popular attractions in the Bayou City. The paved sidewalks are wide and well-landscaped, winding through the zoo in a logical fashion (something

Rare red panda at Houston Zoo.
Photo courtesy Houston Zoo

not all zoos do). Restrooms and snackbars are scattered throughout. Many of the exhibits are open-air enclosures, so you can see elephants or tigers or spectacled bears in their natural habitats. One of the areas not to miss is the World of Primates where a variety of boardwalks and tree houses allow you to observe the behavior of endangered primates like Bornean orangutans, siamangs, mandrills and many, many others. And don't miss the rare red panda. A nice feature about the zoo, especially if you are bringing children, is the daily Meet the Keeper Talks, during which all sorts of up-close-and-personal information about one of the animals is shared. A keeper is talking about every 30 minutes. A new African Forest section opened in 2010. Zoo admission is free on Martin Luther King Day, Presidents Day, Columbus Day, the Friday after Thanksgiving, and New Year's Day.

Needville—Brazos Bend State Park

Trail: 40-Acre Lake Trail
Length: 1.25 miles/easy
Location: 28 miles southwest of Houston.
Information: 21901 Farm Road 762, Needville, TX 77461, 979-553-5102, tpwd.texas.gov/state-parks/brazos-bend
Best Time to Visit: Anytime, but summers are hot.
Why Go: Not far from Houston is a nature-lover's dream. It's isolated from the big city, and you can spy all sorts of birds, check out wildlife, including a rather large number of alligators, and even peek at the heavens at the park's observatory. The 40-Acre Lake Trail follows the banks of a shallow, marshy

Alligator at Brazos Bend State Park.
© Brian Frazier, TPWD

lake and offers views of different aquatic habitats. Some of the walk is shaded, some exposed to full sun. At the southern end of the trail, near the parking area, is an observation deck that juts out over the lake. At the northern end of the loop, is a four-story observation tower that offers commanding views. Almost any time you stroll around here, you'll see some sort of wildlife, whether it's egrets or ducks or bobcats or alligators. The gators are so prolific that the park has warning signs with instructions on how to deal with them. This walk is the best place to see alligators in the park, just make certain to go as early in the morning as possible, when they're more active. Restrooms, a vending machine, and a playground are located at the trailhead. And that low thrumming you occasionally hear on your walk? Those are the gators.

Pasadena—Armand Bayou Nature Center

Trail: Karankawa Trail
Length: 1.5 miles/easy
Location: 8500 Bay Area Blvd., near Clear Lake City.
Information: P.O. Box 58828, Houston, TX 77258, 866-417-3818, www.abnc.org
Best Time to Visit: 9 a.m. to 5 p.m. Tuesdays through Saturdays, noon to 5 p.m. Sundays. (Last admission to trails at 4 p.m.) Avoid the summertime heat and mosquitoes.
Why Go: Get reconnected with nature in the middle of one of the largest urban areas in the nation. To get to this walk, you will drive through some thick traffic and sprawling development—and the Houston Space Center is right around the corner. But once you get here you will be in 2,500 acres of true wetlands prairie and marsh wilderness. This walk is in the heart of a bayou

Pasadena's Armand Bayou Nature Center.
Photo by Allan C. Kimball

ecosystem that once dominated this area of Texas before it was overtaken by the growth of the Houston area with its strip malls and highways. The trail winds through the forested wetlands and is exceptionally quiet except for the singing of birds and insects. The path begins behind the Interpretive Center, which is a different building from the park's headquarters and gift shop. The wide gravel trail is easy to follow and has many shaded benches. About midway you'll find a bayou overlook with another overlook farther north at the park's boat shed. These spots are where you're most likely to see alligators early in the morning and birds like egrets and herons about anytime. Also, if you're so inclined, the Nature Center offers night hikes once a month so you can get a chance to spy on critters that only show themselves after dark.

Rio Hondo—Laguna Atascosa National Wildlife Refuge

Trail: Lakeside Trail
Length: 1.5 miles/easy
Location: Off Texas 106, 14 miles east of Rio Hondo.
Information: P.O. Box 450, Rio Hondo, TX 78583, 956-748-3607, http://www.fws.gov/refuge/laguna_atascosa/
Best Time to Visit: Spring is best for wildflowers and birds.
Why Go: The Texas Gulf plains landscape is a unique blending of temperate, subtropical, coastal, and desert habitats. Mexican plants and wildlife are at the northernmost edge of their range, while migrating waterfowl and sandhill cranes fly down for the mild winters. This combination makes Laguna Atascosa National Wildlife Refuge world famous for its birds and home to a mix of wildlife found nowhere else. The Lakeside Trail starts at Osprey Overlook on the Laguna Atascosa. Views of the lake and thorn forest provide the possibility of good birding. Wildflowers are plentiful, especially during March and April. When you're done walking, head on over to the Alligator Pond. Alligator watching has become very popular at the refuge. During wet years, they seem to inhabit every pond. Alligator Pond, a quarter-mile south of Osprey Overlook, usually has a gator or two. They can also sometimes be seen on the resaca on Lakeside Drive. Alligators can be dangerous; do not feed or annoy them. Keep a close eye on small children and pets.

Port O'Connor—Matagorda Island Wildlife Management Area

Length: 2 miles/easy

Location: Headquarters is about 11 miles southwest of Port O'Connor.

Information: 1700 7th St., Room 101, Bay City, TX 77414, 979-244-7697, tpwd.texas.gov/matagordaisland

Best Time to Visit: Anytime, but summers can be hot and humid and full of mosquitoes.

Why Go: Here's another walk on the beach. This one is very secluded because the only way you can get onto the island is by boat—your own or charter a ride. You can see an 1850s-era lighthouse at the north end of the island where the walk begins at the park headquarters, where you'll also find restrooms and showers. Just wander on down over the dunes onto the beach and walk a mile or two. The 38-mile-long barrier island has a wide variety of migratory birds, many of them endangered, a herd of white-tail deer, and multitudes of alligators along with other wildlife. The southern tip of the island is a common area to see rare whooping cranes.

Sugar Land—Memorial Park

Trail: Park Trail

Length: 2.5 miles/easy

Location: 15300 University Blvd., Sugar Land

Information: City of Sugar Land Parks and Recreation Department, 200 Matlage Way, Sugar Land, TX 77478, 281-275-2885. www.sugarlandtx.gov

Best Time to Visit: Anytime.

Why Go: This is your basic walk in the park—nothing spectacular, but a nice, quiet stroll in pleasant surroundings. The 420-acre park edges the Brazos River, one of the most historic in Texas (native Texans say newcomers can't become real Texans until they are baptized in the Brazos). The walkway is an 8-foot-wide gravel trail. The trail is two loops at the north and south ends of the park connected to each other. The north trail loops around a small lake. Park at either loop. The park was once farmland stripped of trees, but is being restored. The city planted 5,000 trees in 2007 to bring back natural oaks and other varieties; 10,000 in 2008.

HILL COUNTRY AND CENTRAL TEXAS

Austin—Lady Bird Lake (formerly Town Lake)

Length: As long as 10 miles/easy
Location: Mopac (Loop 1) to Congress Avenue.
Information: Austin Parks and Recreation Department, 200 S. Lamar Blvd., Austin, TX 78704, 512-974-6700, www.ci.austin.tx.us/parks/trails.htm
Best Time to Visit: Anytime
Why Go: The gravel trail around the lake is nicely landscaped and relatively flat. It's also the most popular walking and jogging trail in the city, so you will almost always be in the company of others. The lake is an impoundment of the Colorado River. You don't have to do the entire trail unless you're feeling energetic. It can be accessed from several bridges over the river, so check the city's map of the trail that's available online. The Austin Nature and Science Center is nearby, as is Zilker Nature Preserve with more trails. Near the trail, you'll also find some of the best restaurants in Austin.

Austin—Wild Basin Preserve

Length: 2.5 miles/easy down, moderate back
Location: 1 mile north of Bee Caves Road on east side of Loop 360.
Information: 805 N. Capital of Texas Highway, Austin, TX 78746, 512-327-7622, www.wildbasin.org
Best Time to Visit: Anytime.
Why Go: Here's a true wilderness right in the heart of a large city. Wild Basin is a beautiful place with a varied landscape, at one point descending to a falls area at Bee Creek that is a peaceful place to relax. The preserve has several trails that are all relatively short and

*Austin's Wild Basin Preserve.
Photo by Allan C. Kimball*

all connect to one another, so get a map and just wander. It's a maze, but you can't make a wrong turn. The trails all go down into canyons, and many areas are through thick woods so the trail is usually shaded. Several markers along the way point out various trees and plants that flourish in the Hill Country and details can be found on an interpretive brochure. The trails have many benches, and the only thing that mars an otherwise perfect experience is the mix of traffic noise with bird songs. One scenic area overlooks the basin that gives the preserve its name, but you'll also see several McMansions clinging to faraway hills.

Bandera—Hill Country State Natural Area

Trail: Cougar Canyon
Length: 2.5 miles/moderate
Location: 45 miles northwest of San Antonio.
Information: 10600 Bandera Creek Road, Bandera, TX 78003, 830-796-4413, tpwd.texas.gov/state-parks/hill-country
Best Time to Visit: Summers can be very hot.
Why Go: This is one of the most pristine places to walk in the Hill Country, a mosaic of rocky hills and a delightful canyon. You'll find lots of oak and cedar trees typical of the Hill Country, along with creeks, springs, and small waterfalls. And this trail features a nice scenic vista of the canyon it's named after. The area is secluded and rugged, and much of it is exposed to the sun, so walking here in the summertime, especially late morning and after, can be brutal. Any other time, however, will be enjoyable. You are unlikely to encounter many other people along your walk. It's one of the least visited state parks in the Hill Country because of a total lack of amenities: You can't get potable water here so you must bring your own.

Bastrop—Bastrop State Park

Trail: Scenic Overlook Trail and Post Oak Spur
Length: 2.5 miles/moderate
Location: 100 Park Rd 1-A. 30 miles southeast of Austin, 1 mile east of Bastrop on Texas 21.
Information: 3005 Texas 21 East, Bastrop, TX 78602, 512-321-2101, tpwd.texas.gov/state-parks/Bastrop
Best Time to Visit: Summers can be very hot and humid.
Why Go: Take a walk into the heart of the Lost Pines of Texas. The trail begins at the scenic overlook that has a massive stone gazebo looking

out over the tall pine forest, then the trail descends into the forest. Tall pines dominate the landscape all around you, closing in at various spots enough to make the claustrophobic nervous. This is nature at its best. The trail is dirt carpeted with pine needles, but it is criss-crossed with tree roots so take care. It can be easy to get lost along the trail, but the park has provided numerous,

Bastrop State Park. Photo by Allan C. Kimball

color-coded metal blazes on the trees to guide you (the Scenic Overlook Trail is red, the Post Oak Spur is gray). The trail is in nearly total shade for its length, and a couple of benches allow you to rest during your up and down trek. At one point is a short trail to a wildlife viewing blind— a great idea but be aware that most wildlife is active only early in the morning and near dusk. The two trails noted here make a loop, with a small portion along Park Road 1A returning you to the parking area. This would be a perfect walk except for the traffic noises that intrude from a nearby highway.

Gorman Falls at Colorado Bend State Park. Photo by Allan C. Kimball

Bend—Colorado Bend State Park

Trail: Gorman Falls

Length: 3 miles round trip/moderate

Location: 28 miles west of Lampasas off Farm Road 580.

Information: Box 118, Bend, TX 76824, 325-628-3240, tpwd.texas.gov/state-parks/colorado-bend

Best Time to Visit: Spring for good flow over waterfall; other times enjoyable.

Why Go: You know this is one of the most remote state parks in Texas when you have to drive several miles on a dirt road just to get to the headquarters. This is one walk with a great payoff—a 60-foot waterfall surrounded by lush vegetation. It's a beautiful sight. In fact, it's the single prettiest spot in the Hill Country, and if you can do just one walk in this region, make it Gorman Falls. If you're observant, you're likely to spot several endangered bird species who call Colorado Bend home including the black-capped vireo, golden-cheeked warbler and, in cooler months, bald eagles. The gravel trail is rocky in many places but usually typical of the Hill Country—wandering up and down small hills, through oak and cedar breaks, and by lots of cactus until you get to the base of the falls, where nearly constant moisture has created a chaotic jungle of trees, vines, grasses, ferns, moss, and other vegetation. The walk is easy going down until you reach the falls area where you have to scramble over slick rocks. The park has cable guides strung up to keep you from falling—use them. What makes the walk moderately strenuous in hot weather is the return when you have to go back up.

Bergheim—Guadalupe River State Park

Trail: River Trail
Length: About 2 miles/easy
Location: Off Texas 46, 4 miles northeast of Bergheim, about 30 miles north of San Antonio.
Information: 3350 Park Road 31, Spring Branch, TX 78070, 830-438-2656, tpwd.texas.gov/state-parks/guadalupe-river
Best Time to Visit: Anytime.
Why Go: Other trails travel through the woods, but the main attraction at this park is the river so take a walk along its banks. The Guadalupe is the favorite stream of Texans for river recreation, whether it be swimming, canoeing, or tubing but this area is more remote than the crowded New Braunfels area. The trail side of the river is a gentle slope dotted with oak trees and bald cypress trees crowding the bank while the opposite bank is a sheer limestone cliff typical of the Guadalupe along most of its route to the Gulf of Mexico. This is an excellent family walk, with enough variety to keep everyone en-

Guadalupe River State Park.
Photo by Allan C. Kimball

tertained, along with many benches and picnic tables. Bring some gear and go fishing if you'd like. If you stay on the trail past the park boundary, you will discover several areas that are great for photographing the river and the huge cypress trees that line its banks.

Bergheim—Honey Creek State Natural Area

Trail: Tour
Length: About 2 miles/easy
Location: Adjacent to Guadalupe River State Park (see above).
Information: c/o Guadalupe State Park, 3350 Park Road 31, Spring Branch, TX 78070, 830-438-2656, tpwd.texas.gov/state-parks/honey-creek

Best Time to Visit: Anytime.
Why Go: Be educated and get some exercise at the same time along this trail. Honey Creek is so primitive, so secluded, that you can only access it on a Saturday morning and then only by participating in an official tour. It's worth it. Most of the trail follows Honey Creek, so thick with vegetation along its banks that the scene looks almost prehistoric. The diversity of habitats is what's so remarkable here, changing dramatically in rather short distances. The guide will explain all the various plants, their range here is remarkable. The trail drops into a canyon thick with trees. The wa-

Honey Creek State Natural Area.
Photo by Allan C. Kimball

ter burbling over the rocky creek, the breezes rushing through the trees, the stunning variety of green are absolute delights.

Boerne—Cibolo Nature Center

Trail: Woodland Loop Trail
Length: About 1.5 miles/easy
Location: 140 City Park Road, off Texas 46 east of downtown Boerne and 30 miles northwest of San Antonio.
Information: P.O. Box 9, Boerne, TX 78006, 830-249-4616, www.cibolo.org

Best Time to Visit: Open 8 a.m. to dusk daily.

Why Go: Go for a walk in the woods on the Cibolo wilderness trails. The small community of Boerne has kept a portion of its land as pristine as possible with some trails, like the Woodland Loop Trail going off along Cibolo Creek and surrounded by thick brush and trees, and others across a prairie or through a marsh. As you walk along this thickly shaded and secluded trail, hearing only birds, the wind, and your feet along the path, you might find it hard to believe you're just a half-hour from the second largest city in Texas. This trail overlooks the creek in several places and accesses it in a couple of locations. You'll find benches and a restroom near the trailhead, not too far from exhibits in the Nature Center. (By the way, the city is pronounced Burny.)

Burnet—Longhorn Cavern State Park

Trail: Tour
Length: 1.5 miles/easy
Location: 6 miles west of U.S. 281 on Park Road 4.
Information: P.O. Box 732, Burnet, TX 78611, 877-441-CAVE (2283), tpwd.texas.gov/state-parks/longhorn-cavern
Best Time to Visit: Tours leave hourly 10 a.m. to 4 p.m. on weekends and holidays and daily from Memorial Day weekend to Labor Day weekend; leave 11 a.m., 1 p.m., and 3 p.m. starting on the Tuesday after Labor through the Friday before Memorial Day. The cavern hosts Saturday concerts in the summer.
Why Go: This is one of the most unique walks in all of Texas and not just because it's in a cave, although that's good enough. Unlike most of the state's other show caves, Longhorn Cavern was formed by an underground river and so for most of its length does not have the familiar stalactite and stalagmite formations. Because of this, the walls are as smooth as marble and just as attractive. Among your discoveries will be Crystal City, an area decorated with calcite crystals, and the Queen's Watch Dog, a formation that looks as if it were carved from the smooth rock but was actually formed by moving

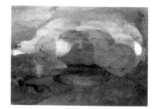

Burnet's Longhorn Cavern State park.
Photo by Allan C. Kimball

water. The Indian Council Room is a large area where Comanche Indians gathered. They were the first to use the cavern. The walk is on a tour, so you are a little limited by when you can go, but the information from the guides is worth it. And if you mispronounce the name of the nearby town, locals will correct you immediately with: "It's Burn-it, durn it."

Concan—Garner State Park

Trail: White Rock Cave and Bird Trail
Length: About 2 miles/strenuous
Location: 31 miles north of Uvalde; 8 miles north of Concan on Ranch Road 1050 off U.S. 83.
Information: 234 Ranch Road 1050, Concan, TX 78838, 830-232-6132, tpwd.texas.gov/state-parks/garner

Concan's Garner State Park.
Photo by Allan C. Kimball

Best Time to Visit: Anytime, although summers can be very crowded.
Why Go: This trail is rocky and very steep in some places, but it's worth the effort. You'll go through thick woodlands with birds singing all around you, and then you're treated to panoramic views of the surrounding hills and the Frio River from several locations. If you just do the White Cave portion, it'll be about a mile round trip, but continue on the Bird Trail to an impressive scenic overlook. If you're still in the mood for exercise, play a round of miniature golf on the park's course. If you happen to be in the park on a summer weekend, take in a dance at the park pavilion or some cowboy poetry and storytelling at the theater. This is one of the most popular parks in Texas, and you'll understand why once you've visited.

Fredericksburg—Downtown

Trail: Shops and Pioneer Museum along Main Street
Length: 1.5 miles/easy
Location: Historic District, along Main Street downtown, from the Nimitz Hotel at Washington Street to Acorn Street.

Information: Fredericksburg Chamber of Commerce, 302 E. Austin St., Fredericksburg, TX 78624, 830-997-6523 or 888-997-3600, www.fredericksburg-texas.com

Best Time to Visit: Anytime.

Why Go: Fredericksburg is one of the most popular towns in the Hill Country, and rightly so. It has an old, rich German tradition, and the shops and restaurants that line Main Street are very distinctive, offering items and fare you simply will not usually find in other towns. And you'll find it difficult to resist sampling something from one of the great German pastry shops or the wine at the family-run winery at the western edge of the shops. The street itself is interesting because it's much wider than streets in other Texas cities its size. Its practical German founders made it doubly wide so wagons could make a U-turn. Along Main, notice that the first letters of the streets crossing to east of the court house spell out ALL WELCOME and those to the west COME BACK. Make sure to visit the Vereins Kirsche Museum across from the courthouse and the Pioneer Museum about a block away. Often, the large lot behind the Vereins Kirsche is host to outdoor shopping and shows during various holidays and Oktoberfest. An award-winning microbrewery, the Fredericksburg Brewing Co., also on Main, serves genuine German-style beers, among others. Local restaurants offer superb wines made locally.

Fredericksburg's Vereins Kirsche Museum.
Photo by Allan C. Kimball

Fredericksburg—Enchanted Rock State Natural Area

Trail: Loop Trail

Length: 4 miles/moderate

Location: 18 miles north of Fredericksburg.

Information: 16710 Ranch Road 965, Fredericksburg, TX 78624, 830-685-3636, tpwd.texas.gov/state-parks/enchanted-rock

Best Time to Visit: Anytime, but summer afternoons on top of the rock can be extremely hot.

Why Go: The most popular trail here goes straight up the face of America's second largest exposed rock—but that's a chore, not a walk. The best walk is on the Loop Trail. Along the way, you'll pass through a couple of different ecosystems, through woods and brush, by a pond, over exposed rock, and you'll see several unusual rock formations that those who do climb the face of

Fredericksburg's Enchanted Rock State Natural Area. Photo by Allan C. Kimball

Enchanted Rock never get to see. Tonkawa Indians gave the rock its name because they believed that ghost fires flickered at the top and they heard strange moaning sounds emanating from the stone. Those sounds can still be heard today at certain times of the night, caused by the rock's heating by day and contracting in the cool of the evening. The rock is a pink granite dome 1,825 feet high, covering 640 acres. Yeah, it's big. If you want to get to the summit, take the Echo Canyon Trail near the end of the Loop Trail that will take you up the back way with much less effort than going straight up the Summit Trail. You should be aware that park staff will close the park once a certain number of cars have been admitted, so go early on weekends.

Ingram—Stonehenge II

Stonehenge II. Photo by Allan C. Kimball

Length: Three-quarters of a mile/easy
Location: Off Texas 39 at the Hill Country Arts Foundation in Ingram.
Information: 120 Point Theatre Road, Ingram, TX 78025, 830-367-5121, www.hcaf.com/index.php/stonehenge-ii
Best Time to Visit: Anytime.
Why Go: If you happen to be driving along in this scenic portion of the Hill Country and not know this place is here, when you

first see it you will be stunned. "What is Stonehenge doing in the middle of Texas?" you will say aloud immediately. Well, it's not the real Stonehenge, of course. That's 3,500 miles away on the Salisbury Plain in England. This is a two-thirds replica made of steel and concrete by Doug Hill and Al Shepperd as a lark after Hill built a patio on Shepperd's home and had some leftover materials. And if the Stonehenge balanced rocks aren't enough to amuse you, the site also features two replicas of the mysterious stone heads found on Easter Island. Roam the property, from one big head to the other, exploring the Stonehenge "rocks" between them.

Johnson City—Pedernales Falls State Park

Trail: Wolf Mountain Trail
Length: 7 miles/easy
Location: 9 miles east of Johnson City off Farm Road 2766.
Information: 2585 Park Road 6026, Johnson City, TX 78636, 830-868-7304, tpwd.texas.gov/state-parks/pedernales-falls
Best Time to Visit: Anytime.
Why Go: The falls here that drop about 50 feet over a distance of 3,000 feet are gorgeous and unusual, especially after spring rains, but that's not where to walk. Check them out after your walk and, if you desire, soak in the cool Pedernales (pronounced Pur-din-alice, by the way) River. The best walk is the easy, seven-mile Wolf Mountain Trail that wraps around Tobacco and Wolf mountains, winding along the small canyons created by Mescal and Tobacco creeks. Stop to cool your heels at Arrowhead Pool, where Bee Creek spills into stair-stepped pools. This is a well-marked trail through oak and juniper woodlands, very typical of the Hill Country. If you happen to be a bird watcher, keep an eye out for the rare golden-cheeked warbler that nests in the park from March through summer.

The falls at Johnson City's Pedernales Falls State Park. Photo by Allan C. Kimball

Luling—Palmetto State Park

Trail: Hiking Trail and Palmetto Trail
Length: 2 miles/easy
Location: 5 miles southeast of Luling off U.S. 183.
Information: 78 Park Road 11 South, Gonzales, TX 78629-5180, 830-672-3266, tpwd.texas.gov/state-parks/palmetto
Best Time to Visit: Anytime.
Why Go: Technically, just east of the Hill Country, you know you're in a special place. As you drive in, the crowns of the trees growing on both sides of the road merge to create a leafy tunnel. Parking in the lot at the 1935

Luling's Palmetto State Park. Photo by Allan C. Kimball

Refectory will give you access to both trailheads. This park on the banks of the San Marcos River features plentiful vegetation and the palmetto or swamp palm. Lots of palmettos. These plants with fanlike leaves rise to about waist high and are everywhere you look. As you might expect, they are abundant on the Palmetto Trail. The Hiking Trail is the longer of the two trails, a wide gravel trail through a thick oak forest with some swampy areas. Pay attention, because more than 240 species of birds have been spotted here, and you're likely to walk by spring wildflowers, see dragonflies flit by and deer rushing through the woods. The Palmetto Trail is even more lush, almost overflowing with palmettos. The feeling is primordial.

Moody—Mother Neff State Park

Trail: Cave Trail
Length: 3 miles/moderate
Location: 16 miles west of Interstate 35, near Moody.
Information: 1680 Texas 236, Moody, TX 76557, 254-853-2389, www.tpwd.state.tx.us/spdest/findadest/parks/mother_neff
Best Time to Visit: Anytime.

Why Go: This was the very first state park in Texas, named for the woman who donated the land, the mother of a Texas governor. What is so nice about this walk is that it is almost completely secluded, going through a thick forest and deep ravines. Just when you begin thinking this area must be one of the most primitive in Texas that was hidden away until it became a park, you come upon signs that people have always enjoyed it. One, at a 40-foot ravine, is the Tonkawa Indian cave that provided shelter and a burial site. Another is a pond used by pioneer women to wash clothing and by the Neff family as a swimming hole. Walk here just once and you'll be back again and again. Just like people have been doing for thousands of years.

New Braunfels—Landa Park

Trail: Panther Canyon Nature Trail
Length: 1.6 miles round trip/moderate
Location: At the intersection of Gazebo Circle and California Street in Landa Park.
Information: New Braunfels Parks and Recreation Department, 424 S. Castell Ave., New Braunfels, TX 78130, 830-221-4000, www.nbtexas.org
Best Time to Visit: Anytime.
Why Go: Panther Canyon is a surprise. It's a true wilderness right in the midst of a city, in a park renowned for its river recreation. This beautiful trail begins at the mouth of Comal Springs and wanders through a heavily shaded

New Braunfels's Panther Canyon in Landa Park. Photo by Allan C. Kimball

narrow canyon. The trees and brush are so thick in the steep canyon that you would likely forget you're surrounded by a city if not for the traffic noise all the time. Because the trail crosses a dry creek bed several times, it has a lot of up-and-down to it, but nothing strenuous although it is routinely rocky. The trail has a number of benches for you to rest on or take in the beauty surrounding you, and has 44 numbered markers locating the various plants in the canyon. The trail ends just past marker 44, so turn around and come back. A number of smaller unofficial trails and game trails converge in this area, but don't take them because they will either get you lost or into someone's backyard.

New Braunfels—Natural Bridge Caverns

Trail: Discovery Tour

Length: 1 mile/moderate

Location: 10 miles north of San Antonio, eight miles west of Interstate 35.

Information: 26495 Natural Bridge Cavern Road, Natural Bridge Caverns, TX 78266, 210-651-6101, www.naturalbridgecaverns.com

Best Time to Visit: Hours vary considerably, but always open 9 a.m. to 4 p.m., later in the summer.

Why Go: This is the largest and best show cave in Texas, with big rooms and spectacular formations, and it's simply one of those attractions you must see. How can you lose? Be entertained, get an education, and get some exercise all at the same time. Descend past the natural bridge into the cavern to a depth of 180 feet. Along the way, you'll see much more than the typical stalactites and stalagmites. You'll spot rock chandeliers, delicate soda straws, and formations that look like a king's throne, a fried egg, or a 50-foot-high watchtower. Pass an underground creek, a 4-foot-deep pile of bat guano, and be awed by the Hall of the Mountain King, an underground chamber so large you could squeeze a football field into it. Guided tours depart from the visitor center every 30 minutes.

Round Mountain—West Cave Preserve

Trail: Tour

Length: 1 mile/easy

Location: Off Hamilton Pool Road, about 40 miles from Austin.

Information: 24814 Hamilton Pool Road, Round Mountain, TX 78663, 830-825-3442, www.westcave.org

Best Time to Visit: Tours at 10 a.m., noon, 2 p.m. and 4 p.m. on weekends.

Why Go: You can only access this trail on guided tours, and then only on weekends, but it's worth it because this is one of the most scenic areas in the Hill Country and one of the most unusual. The trail descends through

Round Mountain's Westcave Preserve. Photo by Allan C. Kimball

grasslands, through thick woodlands, by giant toppled rocks, into a limestone canyon to a collapsed grotto with a 40-foot waterfall tumbling over it into an emerald pool. As if that weren't enough, the waterfall is backed by caves. An Environmental Learning Center is at park headquarters. One important note: The tours are limited to 30 people at a time so you may want to arrive early. Another, larger, collapsed grotto is just up the road at Hamilton Pool Park, which allows swimming and hiking along the Pedernales River.

San Marcos—River Walkway

Length: 2 miles round trip/easy
Location: Begins at the pedestrian bridge in San Marcos Plaza.
Information: San Marcos Chamber of Commerce, P.O. Box 2310, San Marcos, TX 78667, 512-393-5900, www.sanmarcostexas.com
Best Time to Visit: Anytime.

San Marcos River Walkway.
Photo by Allan C. Kimball.

Why Go: This meandering trail follows the beautiful San Marcos River through several parks and a wildlife habitat. The river is one of the best in the state—spring-fed, crystal clear, a constant 72 degrees, and home to unique species of amphibians, fish, insects and plants, some found nowhere else in the world. Not only is the natural scenery along the river gorgeous most of the year, but in warm weather you can also watch hundreds of people canoeing, kayaking and tubing along the river. One of the unique features of the walkway is that you can access an island in the middle of the stream over a footbridge—then relax on one of the two benches on the island. If you're walking in the summertime and want to cool off, take a bathing suit and jump in the river or the city pool at Rio Vista Park. Restrooms are also at Rio Vista. When you reach Cheatham Street, the trail continues into the Wildlife Habitat. You will also discover dozens of bathing-suited college students on the walkway and in the parks. You can extend the walk by following a trail into Lucio Park, with its baseball and softball diamonds, along the feeder for Interstate 35. Park behind the Chamber of Commerce at 202 N. C.M. Allen Parkway.

Smithville—Buescher State Park

Trail: Hiking Trail and Pine Gulch Trail
Length: 2.5 miles/moderate
Location: On Park Rd. 1E, 2 miles northwest of Smithville off Farm Road 153.
Information: 100 Park Rd 1E, Smithville, TX 78602, 512-237-2241, tpwd.texas.gov/state-parks/buescher
Best Time to Visit: Avoid summer.
Why Go: Buescher State Park is adjacent to Bastrop State Park (see above) and even if you don't walk here, you should follow the 12-mile Park Road 1C that connects the two. It's easily the most scenic drive in Texas, going through the heart of the Lost Pines. The prime attraction at Buescher is Park Lake, but the park also has a relatively short interconnected trail system. The

Buescher State Park. Photo by Allan C. Kimball

first portion of the Hiking Trail just follows a utility right-of-way and it's all open to the sun and pretty boring. To avoid that, park at the small lot across from the University of Texas Science Park along Park Road 1C and access the trail there. Follow the Hiking Trail to the Pine Gulch Trail and connect back to the Hiking Trail and return. Ask for a Buescher Hiking Trail map at park headquarters to see where to park and how the trails connect. The trails are more open than those at nearby Bastrop State Park, with more oaks than pines, but are still lovely. The Pine Gulch portion has a lot of small hills.

Vanderpool—Lost Maples State Natural Area

Trail: Maple Trail and portion of East Trail
Length: 2 miles/easy
Location: 5 miles north of Vanderpool.
Information: 37221 Farm Road 187, Vanderpool, TX 78885, 830-966-3413, tpwd.texas.gov/state-parks/lost-maples

Vanderpool's Lost Maples State Natural Area.
Photo by Allan C. Kimball

Best Time to Visit: Fall for best leaf colors, but good anytime.

Why Go: Leaf peepers and bird watchers will love the Maple Trail in the fall. It follows one bank of the Sabinal River while the East Trail follows the other. The Maple Trail then connects with the East Trail. When the Maple Trail ends, continue north to follow the East Trail to the first restroom area, then come back along the opposite river bank for a very nice, varied walk. If you continue along the East Trail from that point, you'll have a moderately strenuous walk of about 5 miles total, so unless you're in the mood for some real exercise, make the turnaround. The Maple Trail cuts through thick stands of maple trees while the East Trail is mostly open. One spot along the Maple Trail has a bench under tall maples that is a great place to take a break and listen to the birds sing, the river burble over rocks, and the rush of the wind.

Waco—Cameron Park Zoo

Length: 1 mile/easy
Location: Off Interstate 35, near University Drive south of downtown.
Information: 1701 N. Fourth St., Waco, TX 76707, 254-750-8400, www.cameronparkzoo.com
Best Time to Visit: 9 a.m. to 5 p.m. Mondays-Saturdays, 11 a.m. to 5 p.m. Sunday.
Why Go: You really don't expect this nice a zoo in such a small city. In addition to all the typical animals you might find in other zoos, it is also home to the rare white rhinoceros. One of the nice aspects of the zoo is the Nature Trail that meanders through trees and away from most of the exhibits, giving you a feeling of solitude. A new feature, Brazos River Country, showcases in seven geographical areas the critters that call Texas home, such as cougars, deer, javelinas, ocelots, bears, and butterflies. One display in this section has large aquariums displaying all sorts of Texas fish as well.

Wimberley—Market Day

Trail: Lions Field
Length: 1.5 miles/easy
Location: At 601 Ranch Road 2325 just north of Wimberley.
Information: Wimberley Lions Club, P.O. Box 575, 512-842-5162, www.shopmarketdays.com
Best Time to Visit: Market Day is the first Saturday of each month March through December.

Wimberley's Market Days.
Photo by Madonna Kimball

Why Go: Thousands of people like to take the walk around Lions Field—it's level, sheltered by all the booths and small buildings, and has all sorts of stuff for sale that you just never knew you couldn't do without. The field is home to Wimberley Market Days, the second largest such event in Texas and the largest in the Hill Country. Begin at Gate 1 on Coyote Trail and wander around to Lion Way at Gate 3. The walkway winds in and around more than 470 booths that vendors fill to overflowing on Market Days. Lions Field can get very crowded—it's one of the more popular destinations in this part of the state—just go a little after daybreak. It'll be cooler in the summer, plus you might find a great bargain then, too. Also at Market Day you'll have your choice of several snack bars for food and refreshments, restrooms, and live music under the pavilion.

NORTH TEXAS

Arlington—Globe Life Ballpark

Trail: Concourse, Walk of Fame, and Legends Museum
Length: 1.5 miles/easy
Location: Just south of Interstate 30 between Dallas and Fort Worth.
Information: 1000 Ballpark Way, Arlington, TX 76011, 817-273-5222, www.texasrangers.com
Best Time to Visit: For game days, consult the schedule on the Web site. Tours and museum hours are 9 a.m. to 4 p.m. Mondays through Satur-

Globe Life Ballpark at Arlington.
Photo by Allan C. Kimball

days, 11 a.m. to 4 p.m. April Sundays through September; 10 a.m. to 4 p.m. Tuesdays through Saturdays October through March (no tours on game days). **Why Go:** Built in 1994, this is one of the best Major League ballparks in America. The 49,115-seat open-air ballpark was designed and constructed with tradition and intimacy in mind with a granite-and-brick facade, exposed structural steel, an asymmetrical playing field, and a home run porch in right field. Look up while walking around the concourse. The architectural details in this ballpark are superb and all Texan, right down to the Lone Stars providing a focal point on each of the exposed steel trusses. An interesting feature of this walk is on a walkway above the concourse: the Walk of Fame. This is a wall on the north and west ends of the ballpark divided into panels marking each year from 1972, the year the Washington Senators moved to Arlington to become the Rangers. Along the concourse, you'll find the Legends of the Game Baseball Museum exhibiting more than 1,000 artifacts of the game from the 19th century to today, including items on loan from the National Baseball Hall of Fame and Museum in Cooperstown. If you go during a game, you'll find food, drink and souvenir concessions everywhere. And, more importantly, if you go during a game you get to watch some Major League Baseball.

Dallas—Arboretum

Length: 2.5 miles/easy
Location: 8525 Garland Rd. in Dallas.
Information: 8525 Garland Rd., Dallas, TX 75218, 214-515-6500, www.dallasarboretum.org
Best Time to Visit: Open daily 9 a.m. to 5 p.m.
Why Go: Something is always blooming at the Dallas Arboretum, one of the best public gardens in Texas. That statement is not made lightly, because this arboretum has lots of competition: San Antonio's Japanese Tea Garden, Forth Worth's Botanic Garden and the Tyler Rose Garden are three top examples. But the Dallas Arboretum is gorgeously land-

Dallas Arboretum.
Photo by Allan C. Kimball**North**

scaped, and its walkway loops around almost perfectly, presenting varying colors and types of plants as you go, all of them identified. The arboretum is so popular that if you go on weekends, you will probably see a wedding or two on the grounds, along with several professional photographers taking portraits with stunning backgrounds. Although most of the trail is a paved sidewalk, you will also find several side bark-covered dirt paths that wind through some of the thicker growth. A portion of the trail is inviting for children, with several exhibits that feature pirate ships and Hansel and Gretel's cottage among others. The arboretum also has several pools and fountains—one pool when viewed from the proper angle appears to be a part of adjacent White Rock Lake. The park has several drinking fountains, restrooms and cafes.

Dallas—Bachman Lake

Trail: Jogging Trail
Length: 3-mile loop/easy
Location: 3500 W. Northwest Highway, west of Love Field, 6.5 miles north of downtown.
Information: Dallas Department of Parks and Recreation, 1500 Marilla St., Room 6FN, Dallas, TX 75201, 214-670-4100, www.dallasparks.org
Best Time to Visit: Anytime, but summers can be very hot so drink lots of water.
Why Go: This may be the most interesting mixture of nature and urban environments in the state. Where else are you going to want to duck as a Southwest airliner drops out of the sky and aims for your head? Well, the big jet isn't really aiming for your head, it's coming in for a landing at adjacent Love Field. The main Southwest runway just happens to end

Dallas's Bachman Lake.
Photo by Madonna Kimball

right at the southeast shore of the lake, so you get a regular up-close-and-personal look at the landing jets. The trail is paved with a mixture of concrete and asphalt and runs through park land around 205-acre Bachman Lake. The trail has many light poles, a playground, restroom, and picnic tables. As the trail meanders along the northern bank, you may see various species of geese and ducks, herons and egrets and seagulls, or a grove of bald cypress trees. Some visitors have even reported seeing otters in the lake. You will also almost always see people rowing sculls on the lake: the Dallas Rowing Club being located on the Shorecrest Drive area of the lake.

Dallas—World Aquarium

Length: 1.5 miles/easy
Location: In the Historic West End District in downtown Dallas.
Information: 1801 N. Griffin St., Dallas, TX 75202, 214-720-2224, www.dwazoo.com/d
Best Time to Visit: Hours 10 a.m. to 5 p.m. daily (closed Thanksgiving and Christmas).

Visitors walk through tunnel below sting rays and sharks. Dallas World Aquarium.
Photo by Madonna Kimball

Why Go: This is an unusual display on three floors of a downtown building of flora and fauna from five continents, 14 countries, three oceans, numerous seas and rivers on three floors. It's not just fish in a tank. In fact, in at least one location, you'll get the feeling that *you* are the one in the tank as you walk through a tunnel with sharks and rays swimming above you. This is really a remarkable experience as you stroll from the Orinoco Rainforest, showcasing various monkeys, manatees, birds and three-toed sloths, over to Mundo Maya with its sharks, reptiles, amphibians, and the unusual black hawk eagle that looks perpetually disturbed. Exhibits highlight the continental shelf, Australia, Japan, Pacific Islands, South Africa, and so much more it's breathtaking. The building is so well designed and exhibits so well constructed that you will soon forget you are inside.

Dallas—Zoo

Length: 2 miles/easy
Location: 3 miles south of downtown, off Interstate 35.
Information: 650 S. RL Thornton Freeway, Dallas, TX 75203, 214-670-5656, www.dallaszoo.com
Best Time to Visit: 9 a.m. to 5 p.m. daily.
Why Go: This zoo—the first in Texas—has a nice selection of exhib-

Dallas Zoo Rhinoceros.
Photo by Allan C. Kimball

its in several main areas, including a children's zoo, on 95 acres. The nicely landscaped, mostly shaded walkway has many benches and vending machines along it. It's also hilly, but that just makes the walk interesting. Many of the exhibits are expansive replicas of natural habitats. The Wilds of Africa area is an extensive exhibit on the various habitats found on that continent, including the rare African penguins. Yes, penguins *do* live in Africa. The zoo is also home to one of the most complete collections of reptiles and amphibians in the nation—many of them rare and exotic. Almost a full third of the zoo is dedicated to children. One of the interesting features there is the Nature Exchange, where kids can take stuff they find in the outdoors (pinecones, for instance) and trade them for other items (maybe a fossil) so they complete a collection.

Fort Worth—Botanic Garden

Trail: Japanese Garden
Length: 1 mile/easy
Location: Just north of Interstate 30 off University Boulevard.
Information: 3220 Botanic Garden Blvd., Fort Worth, TX 76107, 817-871-7686, www.fwbg.org
Best Time to Visit: Anytime, but the area is overwhelmed with colorful blooms in spring, and golds and

Fort Worth Botanical Gardens' Japanese Gardens.
Photo by Madonna Kimball

reds of Japanese maple leaves in the fall. 9 a.m. to 7 p.m.

Why Go: This is the oldest botanic garden in Texas, with more than 2,500 species of native and exotic plants growing in 23 gardens on 109 acres. You can wander several gardens, but the best walk here—one of the best walks in all the Metroplex—is in the Japanese Garden. This area gorgeously landscaped with brooks, ponds, shrines, stones, bridges, trees, and flowers. Everywhere you walk, everywhere you look is in perfect harmony. The garden is so serene, so seductive that you will not want to leave, so after you walk in one direction, take a break and walk again in the opposite direction. You're sure to notice something you missed the first time.

Fort Worth—Zoo

Fort Worth Zoo Orangutan.
Photo by Madonna Kimball

Length: 1.5 miles/easy
Location: Just south of Interstate 30 in Fort Worth.
Information: 1989 Colonial Parkway, Fort Worth, TX 76110, 817-759-7555, www.fortworthzoo.com
Best Time to Visit: Hours vary considerably: consult the Web site.
Why Go: Sure, you can see alligators at many other zoos, but where else can you see the sorts of things found in a gator's stomach like shotgun shells, sneakers, and beer cans? This zoo is kid friendly with an entire meerkat village that will entertain people of all ages. A replica Texas town at one end has natural and cultural history exhibits and pizza and barbecue cafes. The walkway is nicely landscaped and has many rest areas. One of the nice touches here is the African Savannah, where you have a bird's-eye view of rhinos and giraffes from an elevated board-walk. Simply one of the top zoos in Texas.

Glen Rose—Dinosaur Valley State Park

Trail: Track Sites 1 and 2 with Nature Trail
Length: 1.5 miles/easy
Location: 1629 Park Rd 59. 4 miles west of Glen Rose off Farm Road 205.
Information: P.O. Box 396, Glen Rose, TX 76043, 254-897-4588, tpwd.texas.gov/state-parks/dinosaur-valley

Best Time to Visit: Anytime.

Why Go: The first things you notice when driving into this park are the huge dinosaurs: a 70-foot apatosaurus and a 45-foot tyrannosaurus rex. While these may be fiberglass replicas, the real things left their footprints in the mud 113 million years ago—what is now bedrock in the Paluxey River. To a scientist, the tracks even tell a story, that of a smaller, carnivorous dinosaur

*Glen Rose's Dinosaur Valley State Park.
Photo by Allan C. Kimball*

stalking a much larger planting-eating dinosaur, very similar to the poses of the replicas by the park gift shop. Because the tracks are partially or completely underwater depending on the weather, you really have to know what to look for to see them. The park provides illustrations at the track sites to help your search. The Nature Trail begins at Track Site 2 and follows the bank of the river to a park campground. The trail is paved and is open in some places, winding through thick stands of cedar and oak in others. When you get to the campground, return to the Site 2 parking lot by taking the short trail at camp site 35 by the amphitheater.

Jacksboro—Fort Richardson State Park

Trail: Lost Creek Nature Trail/Rumbling Spring Path
Length: 1.5 miles/easy
Location: Off U.S. 281, half-mile south of Jacksboro.
Information: 228 Park Road 61, Jackboro, TX 76458, 940-567-3516, tpwd.texas.gov/state-parks/fort-richardson
Best Time to Visit: Anytime.
Why Go: The landscape around Jacksboro is typical of the eastern edge of the Panhandle: relatively flat and nonexceptional. But Fort Richardson is gorgeous. It has a small lake near park headquarters and several nice walks. The nature trail that travels alongside Lost Creek is a delight. The walkway is beautiful with carefully carved stones and steps. The stone walk gives way to flat dirt in the middle, then returns to the stones again. The trail goes through thick stands of oak punctuated with prickly

Jacksboro's Fort Richardson State Park.
Photo by Allan C. Kimball

pear cactus. Even though you are rarely ever a stone's throw from the creek, you wouldn't know it is there because the oaks are so dominant. You really don't expect this quality of a walk at a historic site. You can make this a loop, and add about a half-mile, if you return along the Rumbling Spring Path that follows the opposite shore of the creek, but the last quarter-mile would be along the paved park road. The Rumbling Spring Path is more rustic than the Lost Creek trail and does provide for a different perspective. Restrooms and a children's playground are near the trailhead.

Meridian—Meridian State Park

Trail: Bosque Trail
Length: 2.5 miles/rating (easy/moderate/strenuous)
Location: 3 miles southwest of Meridian off Texas 22.
Information: 173 Park Road 7, Meridian, TX 76665, 254-435-2536, tpwd.texas.gov/state-parks/meridian
Best Time to Visit: Anytime, but spring is best.
Why Go: Walk where the native Tonkawa and Tawakoni peoples walked, but they didn't have this 72-acre lake. That was created by the Civilian Conservation Corps during the 1930s by damming Bee Creek. The park is thickly wooded with the typical central Texas cedar and oak trees and abundant plants. The Bosque Trail is a little inconvenient because it's not a full loop, so you probably need to figure in another half-mile on a paved road to return to your starting point. But the trail circles Lake Meridian, so it's always just a little bit cooler in the summer, plus you have the option of just jumping in the refreshing waters if you get a little too hot. Although you can have a good time anytime of the year, spring is best because wildflowers are everywhere, and it's the best time to spot the rare golden-cheeked warbler flying through the cedar breaks.

Waxahachie—Gingerbread Trail and Courthouse

Trail: Between Waters and Rogers streets and the old train depot
Length: About 1 mile/easy
Location: Downtown.
Information: Waxahachie Chamber of Commerce, 102 YMCA Drive, Waxahachie, TX 75165, 972-937-2390, www.waxahachiedowntown.com/gingerbread.htm

Waxahachie's Ellis County Courthouse. Photo by Allan C. Kimball

Best Time to Visit: Anytime, but the official Tour of Homes takes place in early June.
Why Go: Waxahachie's "gingerbread" isn't edible—it's slang for the ornate architectural decorations on most of the city's Victorian-style homes. This walk isn't specifically marked, just wander around the main streets and some of the side streets and be amazed that all these old homes are still standing. Go west on Main Street to Grand Avenue to add more mileage and stop by the art museum and library, and even more old homes. The centerpiece of all of this is the incredible Ellis County Courthouse in the middle of downtown. Built in 1894, this pink granite Romanesque building is the best courthouse in Texas. Take the time to check out all the ornate hand-carved decorations on columns, arches, and walls. The carvings have an interesting history: Ask one of the shop owners around the square for details.

PANHANDLE AND HIGH PLAINS

Amarillo—Amarillo Zoo

Length: 1 mile/easy
Location: In Thompson Park at 24th Avenue and U.S. 287.
Information: Amarillo Zoo, Northeast 24th and Dumas Highway, Amarillo, TX 79105, 806-381-7911, www.amarillozoo.org
Best Time to Visit: 9:30 a.m. to 5:30 p.m. Tuesday-Sunday

Bison at the Amarillo Zoo.
Photo by Allan C. Kimball

Why Go: Lions and tigers and bears—oh, yeah. You'll see them along with prairie dogs, leopards, coatimundis, pythons, geckos, spider monkeys, wallabies, and hissing cockroaches. A nice touch is that the zoo also exhibits animals native to this area of Texas like bison, bobcats, coyotes, deer, donkeys, goats, mustangs, and longhorns. Founded in 1955, the zoo covers just 15 acres featuring 45 species of animals, but is gearing up for expansion. It is a small zoo in a small city, but it's free. The zoo is in Thompson Park, adjacent to a playground and picnic areas and near Wonderland Amusement Park.

Amarillo—Medipark Lake

Trail: Lakeside loop
Length: 2 miles/easy
Location: Along Wallace Street between 9th and Hagy streets.
Information: Amarillo Convention and Visitor Council, 1000 S. Park St., Amarillo, TX 79101, 800-692-1338, www.visitamarillotx.com.
Best Time to Visit: Anytime, dawn to dusk.
Why Go: This park is one of the best-kept secrets in Amarillo. It doesn't even have a sign. Most people don't even know its name. The lake is between the Harrington Regional Medical Center north of I-40 and the Don Harrington Discovery Center and has a paved, mostly shaded, walkway around it. Like many city walks, it is not spectacular but is a very pleasant place to walk. The lake is stocked, and you will always find people fishing from the shore—and you'll always find folks striding along the walkway. No swimming, however. The park also has many benches, a children's playground, and a tennis court.

Amarillo's Medipark Lake.
Photo by Allan C. Kimball

Canyon—Palo Duro Canyon State Park

Trail: Lighthouse Trail
Length: 5.75 miles round trip/moderate
Location: 12 miles east of Canyon, off Texas 217.
Information: 11450 Park Road 5, Canyon, TX 79015, 806-488-2227, tpwd.texas.gov/state-parks/palo-duro-canyon
Best Time to Visit: Avoid summer.

Why Go: As they say locally, "Welcome to the Grand Canyon of Texas." Now, that's a slight Texas exaggeration because Palo Duro doesn't have the drama of Arizona's most famous canyon, but its 20,000 acres are unusual and interesting in their own right. And pretty impressive. The canyon is 120 miles long, 20 miles wide and 800 feet deep, located at the edge of the Llano Estacado—the staked plains that define the word "plain." Make sure to take in the scenery at the Visitors Center before heading down the trail. This particular trail is a long one, but worth the walk because it takes you to the Lighthouse, an extraordinary formation of multihued rock out in the middle of no place. This is a grand old walk that will take you back in time. Some of the rocks you'll see in the canyon are 250 million years old. I consider it the best in the region.

Canyon—Panhandle-Plains Historical Museum

Length: 1.25 miles/easy
Location: On Fourth Avenue in Canyon.
Information: 2503 Fourth Ave., Canyon, TX 79015, 806-651-2244, www.panhandleplains.org
Best Time to Visit: Hours vary, so check their Web site.
Why Go: Opened in 1933, this is the state's largest history museum and will take you from pterosaurs to the petroleum industry. In one room is a tyrannosauros rex skeleton, poised and ready to strike, while almost around the corner is a crusty old oil well derrick and antique truck. The petroleum exhibits are all-encompassing, showing you exactly how oil

is discovered and brought to the surface and shipped. Their display of downhole tools is extensive. Their firearms exhibit is comprehensive and includes the actual Sharps rifle Billy Dixon used to make his famed 1,028-yard shot during the Second Battle of Adobe Walls just down the road in 1874. And the large *Amarillo Globe-News* exhibit shows the history of how news used to be gathered. Other areas showcase the native peoples who originally settled in the area and the pioneers who followed them. One nice touch are several exhibits that keep everyday items in a historical perspective, showing how people have carried water from pottery to gourds to canteens to water bottles, or footwear from moccasins to high-button shoes to

Canyon's Panhandle-Plains Historical Museum.
Photo by Allan C. Kimball

rhinestone-encrusted formal slippers. You can even walk along the boardwalks of a life-size 1880s frontier town and see one of the finest Southwest art collections.

Lubbock—Prairie Dog Town at Mackenzie Park

Trail: Prairie Dog Town
Length: Three-fourths of a mile/easy
Location: At 4th Avenue and the Interstate 27 feeder road.
Information: Lubbock Parks and Recreation, 1625 13th St., Lubbock, TX 79401, 806-775-3664, www.mylubbock.us/departmental-websites/departments/parks-recreation/home
Best Time to Visit: Anytime, dawn to dusk.
Why Go: Prairie dogs are endlessly fascinating. This particular town was established with four prairie dogs and two burrows in the 1930s and has thrived. Each town consists of hundreds of burrows: tiny apartments housing a family of two adults and several youngsters. You'll almost always see a sentinel standing on his hind legs, nearly motionless, guarding the entrance to the burrow from predators. These cute critters make highpitched yipping barks and are mas-

ter ditch diggers. Spend any time watching them and one is certain to duck down into a hole and throw up clouds of dirt faster than you can imagine possible. Technically, these are just large ground squirrels, but once you attach the "prairie dog" moniker on , they become something special. Stroll around the town and catch the various animals from every angle. They aren't limited to this little enclave, either. You'll find their burrows dotting the golf driving range adjacent to the town as well. No reports on whether they steal errant golf balls, though.

Lubbock—Walk of Fame

Length: Half a mile/easy
Location: At 8th Street and Avenue Q.
Information: Lubbock Memorial Civic Center, 1501 Mac Davis lane, Lubbock, TX 79401, 806-775-2242, www.civiclubbock.com/walk.html
Best Time to Visit: Anytime.
Why Go: You can't miss this little park in front of the Lubbock Memorial Center thanks to the distinctive Buddy Holly statue right in the middle. Holly, perhaps Lubbock's most famous son, was one of the pioneers of rock and roll. He was honored by this statue in 1979. Since then plaques have been added around the base and on other walls honoring other actors, artists, entertainers, and musicians—like Barry Corbin and Lloyd Maines—who called this area of the Panhandle home. At one end is a fountain honoring the 26 people who died in the 1970 tornado here. It's a pleasant little walk with lots of shade and benches.

Buddy Holly statue at Lubbock's Walk of Fame. Photo by Allan C. Kimball

Quanah—Copper Breaks State Park

Trail: Equestrian Trail
Length: 1.5 miles/easy
Location: 12 miles south of Quanah off Texas 6.
Information: 777 Park Road 62, Quanah, TX 79252, 940-839-4331,

tpwd.texas.gov/state-parks/copper-breaks

Best Time to Visit: Avoid summers.

Why Go: This area was important to the Comanches and Kiowas. Cynthia Ann Parker, who was captured and raised by Comanches, was recaptured near the current park area. Her son, Quanah Parker, was the last war chief of the Comanches, and the nearby town is named for him. This is a remote park that's far less crowded than parks near larger urban areas. It's a semi-arid region of brush, grasses, cottonwoods, pecans, mesquite-covered mesas and cedar breaks. The trail circles Big Pond, sometimes close to it and often quite a distance removed. On the shores of the pond, you will spot herons and egrets, and farther away you'll find interesting hills of red and white earth typical of this neck of the woods. If you know what to look for, you'll also see layers of copper peeking through the ground—that and the surrounding thick brush (called "breaks" in Texas) give the park its name.

Quitaque—Caprock Canyon State Park

Trail: Haynes Ridge Overlook
Length: 5 miles round trip/moderate
Location: 850 Caprock Canyon Park Rd.
Information: P.O. Box 204, Quitaque, TX 79255, 806-455-1492, tpwd.texas.gov/state-parks/caprock-canyons
Best Time to Visit: Anytime, but spring is best.

Why Go: Except for Big Bend Ranch State Park, you won't find any place that feels more desolate than this trail. It's also not what you might expect from a place in the middle of the Staked Plains. It's not flat. It provides you with engaging vistas of the North and South forks of the Red River and the surrounding canyonlands. It gives you the opportunity to see buffalo in the wild. And if you can't find lizards to play with, you're not trying. The trail is a little strenuous as you gain elevation, but

Aerial view of Caprock Canyon State Park.
© *Earl Nottingham, TPWD*

most of it is flat and quite easy. Although the trail can be enjoyed any-time, in spring you can have clear skies and the surrounding red beds of mudstones, sandstone, shales, and siltstones are dotted with deep green vegetation. Erosion has modified the colors into various shades of red and orange, even white. The overlook is toward the eastern end of the trail and can be quite breezy. These scenic canyons were home for Native Americans of many cultures for thousands of years, the most recent were Comanches. The park is on land once owned by famed cattleman Charles Goodnight and it's the descendants of his bison you'll run into. By the way, locals pronounce Quitaque "kitty-kway."

SOUTH TEXAS

Brownsville—Gladys Porter Zoo

Length: 2.5 miles/easy
Location: 500 Ringgold St. in Brownsville.
Information: 500 Ringgold St., Brownsville, TX 78520, 956-546-7187, www.gpz.org
Best Time to Visit: 9 a.m. to 5:30 p.m. weekdays, 9 a.m. to 6 p.m. weekends.
Why Go: This zoo isn't the largest in Texas, but it is one of the very best. Encompassing, 31 acres of lush tropical plants and 1,600 animals, it is re-nowned for its successes in breeding endangered species. All but a couple of the animal exhibits are open air-sites where the animals can run free in settings that resemble their natural habitats.

Lion at Brownsville's Gladys Porter Zoo. Photo by Madonna Kimball

In fact, rather than look at birds in a cage, you can enter the cage and have birds flit all about you. Buy a stick with seeds before you enter, and the birds will eat out of your hand. The walkway is the most beautifully land-scaped of any zoo in the state with much of it deeply shaded with several benches along the way. Among the rare animals you will see are the bontebok, pygmy hippopotamus, duiker, gaur, white rhinocerous, and siamang. The most popular exhibit is probably the gorillas: Lamydoc and Katanga have been at the zoo for more than 30 years, producing three generations of gorillas.

Brownsville—Resaca de la Palma State Park

Trail: Kiskadee Trail and Mexican Olive Trail
Length: 1.5 miles/easy
Location: 1000 New Carmen Road, about 4 miles southwest of Olmito off Farm Road 1732 from U.S. 83.
Information: P.O. Box 714, Olmito, TX 78575, 956-350-2920, www.theworldbirding center.com/Resaca.html
Best Time to Visit: Anytime, but birding is best in mid-spring and mid-fall.
Why Go: This is one of Texas' newest state parks and the largest tract (1,200 acres) in the World

*Brownsville's Resaca de la Palma State Park.
Photo by Allan C. Kimball*

Birding Center network of refuges in the Lower Rio Grande Valley. A *resaca* is a dry river bed that fills during rainy periods, attracting birds and animals. The park was designed to restore these wetlands to their primitive state so vehicles are banned. To access trails, you must either walk, take a tram, or rent a bicycle. Each trail noted has an observation deck that overlooks a *resaca* that is usually full of waterfowl. The trail goes through typical South Texas brush country, and you're likely to spot several other birds like mockingbirds and kites, vireos and thrashers. The one that seems like a flash of bright yellow in the corner of your eye is the altamira oriole. Look for their unusual hanging nests along the trails.

Edinburg—Edinburg Scenic Wetlands

Length: 2 miles/easy
Location: 714 S. Raul Longoria Rd. in Edinburg.
Information: Edinburg Parks and Recreation Department, P.O. Box 1079, Edinburg, TX 78540, 956-381-9922, www.worldbirdingcenter.org and www.edinburgwbc.org
Best Time to Visit: Anytime, dawn to dusk. Spring is best for wildflowers.
Why Go: Part of the World Birding Center, Edinburg Scenic Wetlands is 40 acres of

*Edinburg Scenic Wetlands.
Photo by Allan C. Kimball*

endangered wetlands with shallow ponds that attract all sorts of creatures, including more than 13 species of ducks in the winter and several bird species found no place else in Texas. The winding trail crosses itself several times, wandering to areas thick with butterflies and to waterside observation platforms. Several unusual trees are marked along the trail: crucillo, Texas ebony, and tepeguaje among them. You'll find many benches from which to listen to all the birds that love this place. The park also has an Interpretive Center with several exhibits. If you're a serious bird watcher, late April and the first week of May are the best times to catch a glimpse of all the migrating flocks.

Goliad—Goliad State Park

Trail: Aranama Nature Trail and River Trail
Length: About 3 miles round trip/easy
Location: A quarter-mile south of Goliad off U.S. 183.
Information: 108 Park Road 6, Goliad, TX 77963, 361-645-3405, tpwd.texas.gov/state-parks/goliad
Best Time to Visit: Anytime.
Why Go: You'll find an unusual blend of cultural, historical, and natural resources at Goliad State Park. It's the home to the Mission Espiritu Santo State Historic Site, and just down the road is the Presidio La Bahia, Ignacio Zaragoza' Birthplace State Historic Site, and the Fannin Battleground State Historic Site. The park is nearly surrounded by the San Antonio River, and the River Trail follows it around from the Aranama Nature Trail. Aranama is beautiful, but a little short. The River Trail winds through thick stands of oak, breaking into open areas

Goliad State Park.
Photo by Allan C. Kimball

with picnic tables and grills in a couple of places. Although the trail is easy to follow, it is not marked, so get a map at park headquarters and ask a staff member where to begin. If you're so inclined, you can access a longer trail from here that will take you to either the impressive Presidio La Bahia or historic downtown Goliad with its lovely courthouse. Goliad is more renowned for its history than nature, so you will likely have the trail mostly to yourself except on weekends.

Mission—Bentsen-Rio Grande Valley State Park

Trail: Hawk Tower and Rio Grande Trail

Length: 2.75 miles/easy

Location: Off U.S. 83, five miles southwest of Mission along the Rio Grande.

Information: 2800 S. Bentsen Palm Drive, Mission, TX 78572, 956-584-9156, www.theworldbirdingcenter.com/Bentsen.html

Best Time to Visit: Anytime. Best for birders are the last week in March and first week in April, along with the last week in September and first week in October.

Why Go: This park has become the headquarters of the World Birding Center which has several sites in the general area. The park is closed to vehicles, so to get to the trails you must either walk about two miles from park headquarters, take the tram, or rent a bicycle. The Hawk Tower is not really a tower; it's more of an elevated walkway with panoramic views of the surrounding brush country and adjacent resaca. The tower is unique, however, in

Hawk Tower at Mission's Bentsen-Rio Grande State Park. Photo by Allan C. Kimball

that when the many species of hawks are migrating through, you might see thousands in a half-hour. The trail is a wide walkway through thick colima, mesquite and tepeguaje brush that gives you shade and protection from the winds. Along the trail you are going to spy many birds, including the noisy chacalaca and beautiful kiskadee. You might even spy a rare jaguarundi darting through the brush. The trail also has an observation deck surrounded by river cane that overlooks the Rio Grande. It gets my vote best in the region.

San Antonio—Japanese Tea Garden

Length: About 1.25 miles/easy

Location: 3853 N. St. Mary's St.

Information: San Antonio Parks and Recreation Department, P.O. Box 839966, San Antonio, TX 78283, 210-207-3000, saparksfoundation.org/japanese-tea-garden/

Best Time to Visit: Anytime, dawn to dusk.

Why Go: Take a walk through a Texas historic landmark, a serene beauty that is also on the National Register of Historic Places. The gardens are adjacent to the San Antonio Zoo, so you can park your car there and wander up the road into the gardens or park at the main garden lot. The gardens were created in 1918 in an old rock quarry, and you can walk above and around them, then down through beautiful floral displays, around ponds, and by a waterfall. These Japanese Gardens don't cover as much ground as the Fort Worth Japanese Garden, but they've been recently renovated and a

San Antonio's Japanese Tea Gardens. Photo by Allan C. Kimball

walk here is just as relaxing. If you walk along the outer roadway, at the top of the hill you'll be treated to a commanding view of the gardens and a panoramic view of downtown San Antonio. It's a city park, so there's no admission.

San Antonio—Market Square

Length: 2.5 miles/easy

Location: Between Commerce and Dolorosa streets just east of Interstate 35 in downtown San Antonio.

Information: Market Square, 514 W. Commerce St., San Antonio, TX 78207, 210-207-8600, www.marketsquaresa.com. Museo Alameda, 210-299-4300, www.thealameda.org

Best Time to Visit: 10 a.m. to 8 p.m. June through August, 10 a.m. to 6 p.m. September through May. The museum is open noon to 6 p.m. Tuesdays through Sundays.

Why Go: Want to visit Mexico but don't want to cross the border? Go to Market Square. This

San Antonio's Market Square. Photo by Allan C. Kimball

is a festive place with several buildings to wander through, each full of vendors, along with a couple of very good restaurants and a new art museum. As you walk, you'll discover hats, caps, pottery, jewelry, T-shirts, dresses, toys, and all sorts of gifts from classy to kitschy. And on weekends you'll be serenaded by live music at different locations. The Museo Alameda presents the Latino experience in the Americas through paintings, photographs, sculpture and collages. It's affiliated with the Smithsonian Institution, so you know it's a first-class museum. Parking is either on the roof of one of the buildings or under the freeway. The distance you walk will increase depending on how many shops you stroll through.

San Antonio—Riverwalk

San Antonio's River Walk.
Photo by Allan C. Kimball

Trail: Loop from the St. Mary's Street intersection with Crockett to St. Mary's at Villita Street.
Length: 3 miles/easy
Location: Downtown San Antonio.
Information: Paseo del Rio Association, 110 Broadway St., Suite 500, San Antonio, TX 78205, 210-227-4261, www.thesanantonioriverwalk.com
Best Time to Visit: Anytime, but very crowded on weekends.
Why Go: Here's the real San Antonio, right along the banks of the San Antonio River, in the shadow of the Alamo. The walk here is well below the downtown streets that surround it, so you will be protected from the sun and wind and most of the traffic noise. This is a very scenic walk along landscaped sidewalks with benches placed in shade at convenient distances. The walk is especially attractive in the spring as all the flowers bloom and around Christmas when the walk is decorated with thousands of lights. Along the walk are dozens of gift shops, several hotels, snack shops, and some of the best restaurants in the city. And because most of the eateries have outdoor patios, you'll also be entertained by the sounds of mariachi music on weekends. The Riverwalk began in 1941 when the tourist potential of the San

Antonio River's banks downtown was realized, and it's operated today as a city park. The walkways continue on much farther than is noted here, so you can make this walk almost any length you would like. Extentions also angle off to the River Center Mall and the Convention Center. Get a map from one of the River Rangers or from the address above.

San Antonio—Zoo

San Antonio Zoo Eagle.
Photo by Madonna Kimball

Length: About 3 miles/easy
Location: At St. Mary's and Tuleta streets.
Information: 3903 N. St. Mary's St., San Antonio, TX 78212, 210-734-7184, www.sazoo-aq.org
Best Time to Visit: 9 a.m. to 5 p.m. daily. Schools often take field trips here on Fridays, so to avoid those crowds you might want to visit on another day.
Why Go: The San Antonio Zoo is one of the oldest, and one of the best, in Texas. The 56-acre zoo is home to more than 3,500 animals, representing 600 species, everything from aardwolves to Zanzibar red bishop birds. The walkways circle around and double back on one another so you can easily lengthen or shorten your walk, depending on the route you take and whether you stroll through the newly renovated aquarium or take a peek at an 8,000-pound hippopotamus lounging underwater at the new Africa Live! exhibit. One pleasant amenity is that everywhere you go is the sound of rushing water either over cascades or in streams. At many of the exhibits, nothing separates you from the animals except a deep moat. This zoo pioneered cageless exhibits, like the Barless Bear Terraces and Primate Paradise, way back in 1929. Admission here is the lowest among major zoos in the state, and many regular walkers take advantage of the low annual membership so they can stroll any day they feel it. Also, unlike many of the other zoos in Texas, parking is free.

West Texas

Abilene—Zoo

Length: 1.5 miles/easy

Location: In Nelson Park, off Texas Highway 36.

Information: 2070 Zoo Lane, Abilene, TX 79602, 325-676-6085, www.abilenetx.com/zoo

Best Time to Visit: 9 a.m. to 5 p.m. daily, 9 a.m. to 9 p.m. Memorial Day and Labor Day.

Why Go: Along this walk, you'll discover 500 animals representing more than 200 species including bears, bison, giraffes, jaguars, black rhinos and zebras, and a diverse selection of birds, primates, and reptiles. You'll also find several aquariums and a butterfly garden. This zoo is an intimate one, where you may feed several of the animals and get rather close to most of them. You'll even find one location, on a walkway over the giraffe enclosure, where you can get face-to-face with that curious long-necked animal. They'll eat animal crackers right out of your hand. This zoo is not as large as many others in Texas, but it's a pleasant location, very affordable, rarely crowded, and a nice walk.

Big Spring—Comanche Trail Park

Trail: Rose Magers Trail and Big Spring trails

Length: 2.5 miles round trip/easy

Location: On Comanche Trail Road off U.S. 87.

Information: Big Spring Parks and Recreation Department, 310 Nolan St., Big Spring, TX 79720, 432-264-2376, www.mybigspring.com/recreation/parks.htm

Best Time to Visit: Anytime, dawn to dusk.

Why Go: This 136-acre park was built by the Civilian Conservation Corps in the 1930s and features a golf course, picnic areas, playgrounds, disc golf course, tennis courts, a lake and a

Big Spring's Comanche Trail Park.
Photo by Allan C. Kimball

swimming pool along with its walking trail. Almost nothing is marked in the park, so after you drive into the first entrance just south of the city, pull into the first parking lot by the picnic tables and you will see the wide gravel trail along the banks of Comanche Trail Lake. Follow the trail around to the big spring the city is named for and wander over the maze of smaller dirt trails through thick cactus and mesquite stands. You can't take a wrong turn, just go exploring. The spring area is gorgeous, and you may want to sit on one of the rocks towering over it and rest, letting your mind wander.

El Paso—Franklin Mountains State Park

Trail: Upper Sunset Trail
Length: 2.6 miles round trip/moderate
Location: Off Transmountain Road in west El Paso.
Information: 1331 McKelligon Canyon Road, El Paso, TX 79930, 915-566-6441, tpwd.texas.gov/state-parks/franklin-mountains
Best Time to Visit: Anytime, but go in spring to see beautiful wildflower and cactus blooms.
Why Go: This is the largest urban park in the country with 24,247 acres. You can be overwhelmed by your choices here and confused by the fact that the main Visitors Center is not in the heart of the park. The Visitors Center is in McKelligon Canyon, the far east end of the park, and is connected to the main area only by a very long, very strenuous trail over the mountains. So visit the center, then drive to the Tom Mays Unit of the park where most of the trails and all the restrooms, camping and RV sites are. The Upper Sunset Trail follows a ridge of the mountains

El Paso's Franklin Mountains State Park.
Photo by Allan C. Kimball

and is relatively level. Park at the end of the road by the picnic tables and wander out and back. The view combines the Chihuahuan Desert below you and the mountains surrounding you. These mountains are jumbles of rock and cactus, rising to over 7,000 feet and offer spectacular views of the valleys all around. Look up, you're likely to see golden eagles and falcons soaring overhead. If you want to see the area from an eagle's point of view, head over to the Wyler Aerial Tramway portion of the park at 1700 McKinley Ave. off Alabama Avenue and take a gander at 7,000 square miles spread out way below you.

El Paso—Hueco Tanks State Historic Site and Park

Trail: Pictograph Trail
Length: 1.5 miles/easy
Location: 32 miles northeast of El Paso off U.S. 61 on Ranch Road 2775.
Information: 6900 Hueco Tanks Rd. 1, El Paso, TX 79938, 915-857-1135, tpwd.texas.gov/state-parks/hueco-tanks
Best Time to Visit: Anytime. Hours of the park and tours vary considerably, so consult the Web site before heading out.
Why Go: Now here are some Cliff notes you won't get in trouble studying. Hueco Tanks abounds in mysterious, sometimes colorful pictographs documenting the travels of prehistoric people who wandered through here in search of water. The most famous of the pictographs are the "masks," the largest assemblage of painted faces in North America. One eerily looks like a bearded hippie, complete with sunglasses and blonde hair. Because vandals have defaced some of the pictographs, access to

El Paso's Hueco Tanks State Historic Site. Photo by Allan C. Kimball

many of them is on guided tours only. It's worth it to take one, but you need to call ahead for reservations. One of the pictograph trails is open daily, however, and gives you the opportunity to discover the hidden art on your own. Look for them on cliff faces, in caves, and under overhangs. You may have to scramble to find some of them, but the effort is worth it. Restrooms are available at the end of the trail. Within the park are historic sites of a pioneer home and a Butterfield Stage station along with four hills of volcanic stones that trap water and create special habitats. The park admits only 70 people at any one time, so come early.

El Paso—McKelligon Canyon Park

Trail: Roadside Trail

Length: 4 miles round trip/easy

Location: Off Alabama Ave. in El Paso (turn in at the McKelligon Canyon Pump Station).

Information: 1500 McKelligon Canyon Drive, El Paso, TX 79902, 915-564-9138, www.visitelpaso.com

Best Time to Visit: Anytime, dawn to dusk.

Why Go: Walk into this beautiful canyon in the heart of the Franklin Mountains. The trail is in a 90-acre city park right in the middle of the city but surrounded on three sides by typical desert mountains and offers seclusion from the urban bustle. Look around and enjoy the sotol, yucca, mesquite, and lots of white wing doves. Park near the amphitheater, where the historical drama *Viva! El Paso* plays from spring to fall.

The amphitheater is in a dramatic side canyon. The trail is paved and runs alongside the road, so just stroll from the parking area to Alabama Avenue and back with all the other walkers. Near the parking area are a number of picnic tables. The Visitors Center for Franklin Mountains State Park is also here, so you can pick up a map of trails for that area while you're there.

El Paso's McKelligon Canyon.
Photo by Allan C. Kimball

El Paso—El Paso Saddleblanket Company

Length: 1 mile/easy

Location: Exit 25 from Interstate 10.

Information: 6926 Gateway East, El Paso, TX 79915, 800-351-7847 or 915-544-1000, www.elpasosaddleblanket.com

Best Time to Visit: 9 a.m. to 5 p.m. Mondays through Saturdays.

Why Go: Here's a walk that's not only a visual treat, but you can also do just about all your shopping while you stroll. El Paso Saddleblanket Company's main showroom is an acre and they've just added another building that measures about the same. Walking up and down the aisles will take you by pottery, rugs, books, serapes, tomahawks, door mats, blankets, arrowheads, spears, powder horns, mandellas, clothing, sheep skins, drums, sand paintings, dream catchers, scorpion paperweights, medicine rattles, cowhides, bullwhips, chaps, hats and sombreros, bows and arrows, several cases of jewelry, an entire wall of spurs, a room full of handmade saddles, and, yes, the best saddle blankets your pony will ever love. In the new building you'll find rustic redwood furniture, stained and natural. If it's Western or Southwestern, you'll find it here. Make a couple trips, because it's likely something was missed the first time around.

Fort Davis—Chihuahuan Desert Nature Center and Botanical Gardens

Trail: Modesta Canyon
Length: 1.75-mile loop/moderate
Location: 4 miles south of Fort Davis on Texas 118.
Information: P.O. Box 905, Fort Davis, TX 79734, 432-364-2499, www.cdri.org
Best Time to Visit: 9 a.m. to 5 p.m. Mondays through Saturdays.
Why Go: At an elevation of 5,040 feet, this facility of the Chihuahuan Desert Research Institute is much cooler in the summer than most places in Big Bend, and if you take the Modesta Canyon walk you will be in complete shade for about half the trip. This trail is more a hike than a walk, but is worth every drop of sweat. This is unquestionably one of the best hikes in the Big Bend area. The canyon is narrow and quite deep with unusual geological formations. The formation along the western wall of the canyon is tilted and broken strata the likes of which you'll rarely ever see. At the bottom of the canyon is a spring-fed pool with crawfish frolicking in it. On the cliffs, you'll notice fairy sword ferns along with typical cactus and one of the largest Texas madrone trees in the state. Make certain to begin the loop by walking down into the canyon, then out along a couple of switchbacks to return along the canyon rim. The trail down is well marked but rocky. An interpretive guide brochure is available at the Visitors Center. Seeing the 20-acre Botanical Gardens in spring for the cactus blooms will add about another mile to your walk.

Fort Davis—Fort Davis National Historic Park and Davis Mountains State Park

Trail: Between Fort Davis National Historic Site and Davis Mountains State Park

Length: 1 mile/strenuous if done as a loop, easy otherwise.

Location: The national park is on Texas 17 just north of downtown Fort Davis. The state park is 4 miles northwest of Fort Davis on Texas 118.

Information: Fort Davis National Historic Site, P.O. Box 1379, Fort Davis, TX 79734, 432-426-3224, ext. 20, ww.nps.gov/foda. Davis Mountains State Park, P.O. Box 1707, Fort Davis, TX 79734, 432-426-3337, tpwd.texas.gov/state-parks/davis-mountains

Fort Davis's Davis Mountains State Park.
Photo by Allan C. Kimball

Best Time to Visit: Anytime. Fort Davis is open 8 a.m. to 5 p.m. daily; closed Thanksgiving, Christmas, New Year's, and Martin Luther King Jr. Day.

Why Go: This is a unique walk, running between the state park and the national park and offering commanding views of each one. The view into the state park includes the Indian Lodge that was built in the 1930s by the Civilian Conservation Corps. Book rooms in the lodge well in advance. The view into the National Park includes Officers Quarters and Enlisted Barracks built just after the Civil War. The site is one of the bestrestored, Indian Wars-era forts in the country. The length of your walk can vary considerably depending on where you start and where you stop, and whether you make it a loop. If you walk between the state park's interpretive center and the bottom of the Hospital Canyon Trail in the national park, the trail is about 3.5 miles one way. If you begin at the end of Skyline Drive in the state park and go to the Scenic Overlook in the national park, it's about two miles round trip.

Lajitas—Big Bend Ranch State Park

Trail: Closed Canyon

Length: 1.5-mile round trip/easy

Location: About 20 miles west of Lajitas on Texas 170 (the River Road).

Information: P.O. Box 2319, Presidio, TX 79845, 432-358-4444, www.tpwd.state.tx.us/spdest/findadest/parks/big_bend_ranch

Best Time to Visit: Anytime, dusk to dawn.

Why Go: Closed Canyon is a fascinating place that draws visitors back time and time again. It's one of the few slot canyons in Texas: The trail follows a dry creek bed from the head of the canyon just off the River Road toward its mouth at the Rio Grande. After parking at the trailhead, look for the big crack in the cliff wall and head for it—that's the canyon, and the trail is not marked except for rock cairns that often get knocked over or washed away. You can't get lost inside the canyon because it's so narrow. The first quarter-mile or so in the canyon is easy going, but then you encounter rocky drops that get steeper the farther in you go. At

Closed Canyon at Big Bend Ranch State Park. Photo by Allan C. Kimball

some point, you cannot go on without climbing equipment or others in your group staying behind with ropes to haul you out. You don't have to go that far, though, to enjoy the unusual formations: steep cliffs on each side that seem to close in on you as you walk in, large veins of calcite in the cliff faces, cactus growing sideways from solid rock faces. It's all quite breathtaking. Just remember that the trail is a dry creek bed, and if it starts to rain you would be wise to get out of the canyon quickly or you might be swept away—those cliffs are high and they are sheer.

Lajitas—Big Bend Ranch State Park

Trail: Barton Warnock Environmental Education Center and Desert Garden

Length: 1 mile/easy

Location: One mile east of Lajitas on Farm Road 170.

Information: HC 70 Box 375, Terlingua, TX 79852, 432-424-3327, tpwd.texas.gov/state-parks/big-bend-ranch

Best Time to Visit: Anytime, but summer afternoons can be brutally hot. 8 a.m. to 4:30 p.m. daily.

Why Go: First, take a walk through the Una Tierra/One Land presentation in several rooms of the Interpretive Center adjacent to the entry building. The various displays chronicle the cultural and natural history of the Big Bend in a comprehensive way, showing off everything from dinosaur bones to old mining photos. Then wander out to the gravel trail through the Desert Garden, 2.5 acres of landscape showcasing all the plants common to the Chihuahuan Desert. In case you wonder what some of them are, they're all labeled. Don't worry, there's no test later. At the end of the garden loop, walk up the steps to a scenic overlook for a dramatic view. You can buy permits for the remainder of your stay in Big Bend Ranch State Park and get maps and other information. In the main building you will also find a comprehensive collection of books about the Big Bend, including *The Big Bend Guide* (by me) that no traveler here should be without.

Langtry—Judge Roy Bean Visitor Center

Trail: Around Museum and Cactus Garden
Length: 1 mile/easy
Location: 60 miles west of Del Rio off U.S. 90 on Loop 25 in Langtry.
Information: Torres Avenue, Langtry, TX 78871, 432-291-3340, 800-452-9292, www.txdot.gov/travel/information_centers.htm
Best Time to Visit: 8 a.m. to 5 p.m., to 6 p.m. between Memorial Day and Labor Day. Closed Easter, Thanksgiving, Christmas Eve, Christmas, and New Year's Day.
Why Go: No other state has a walk like this, but then no other state ever had a justice of the peace like Judge Roy Bean, who dispensed his roughshod brand of justice at his Jersey Lilly Saloon in the late 1800s. The saloon, its adjacent billiard hall and Bean's home are preserved by the Texas Travel Information Center in this remote community along the Rio Grande. Start your walk inside the Travel Center where you can pick up a wealth of free literature and information for just about any destination in the Lone Star State. Among the displays, you'll see Judge Bean's copy of the 1879 Revised Statutes of Texas and the pistol he used as a gavel to bring law to this area west of the Pecos. Continue on to the six dioramas that tell the judge's unusual story, then head outside to the Jersey Lilly—named after famed actress Lillie

Famed Jersey Lilly Saloon at the Judge Roy Bean Visitor Center. Photo by Allan C. Kimball

Langtry whom Bean erroneously thought the town was named after (it was actually named for George Langtry, a railroad civil engineer). Wander the ramshackle gin mill and billiard hall, then check out Bean's home. Finally, stroll through the Cactus Garden, where you'll discover agave, beargrass, cholla, devil's pincushion, guayule, huisache, prickly pear, rougeplant, Spanish yucca, tasajillo, wild china, and yaupon among many other plants and trees you're likely to see here in the Chihuahuan Desert. The windmill is pretty cool, too.

Muleshoe—Muleshoe National Wildlife Refuge

Trail: Nature Trail
Length: 2 miles round trip/easy
Location: 20 miles south of Muleshoe off Texas 214 on Caliche Road.
Information: P.O. Box 549, Muleshoe, TX 79347, 806-946-3341, www.fws.gov/refuge/muleshoe/
Best Time to Visit: Fall and winter.
Why Go: This is the oldest national wildlife refuge in Texas. It's along the Central Flyway bird migration route, so in spring and fall, you'll see a huge number of birds, including Canada geese, sandhill cranes and various ducks and herons. If you get lucky, you might even spot a rare whooping crane. They're attracted here by the water—the refuge has four lakes. Three of the lakes depend on rainfall, but Upper Paul's Lake is spring fed. Prairie dogs are common, but so are rattlesnakes, so watch out. The trail follows an arroyo alongside Upper White Lake, which is a favorite of passing cranes as long as the lake doesn't get too deep. About midway, the Nature Trail takes you to an overlook of the lake. When you get near the overlook, be quiet and move slowly because if you frighten the birds, they will all fly off. If your goal is birding, check with park headquarters for locations on several observation points that don't require walking.

Odessa—Memorial Gardens

Trail: Buffalo Wallow
Length: 1 mile/easy
Location: 473 E. 42nd St., across from Music City Mall in Odessa.
Information: Odessa Parks and Recreation, 1100 W. 42nd St., Odessa, TX 79761, 432-368-3548, www.odessa-tx.gov/

Best Time to Visit: Anytime, dawn to dusk.

Why Go: The only buffalo you'll see here now are of the bronze variety, and any real ones would marvel at the lake that has replaced the depression in the ground where they used to roll around in the dirt to rid themselves of pests or shed their winter coats in the spring. This is now a nice pedestrian park with a paved trail that encircles the small lake, featuring many bronze statues, a fountain, and a waterfall along the way. One nice touch is the "pooch station" near the trailhead with plastic baggies and a trash can to help you clean up after your dog. Unfortunately, the numerous ducks who love the lake don't clean up after themselves, so be careful where you walk in certain areas. The park becomes an amazing spectacle on Sept. 11, when volunteers raise hundreds of full-size American flags to commemorate those who died in the 2001 terrorist attacks.

Odessa—Meteor Crater

Length: 1 mile round trip/easy

Location: 10 miles southwest of Odessa off Interstate 20 on Meteor Crater Road.

Information: 432-381-0946, www.netwest.com/virtdomains/meteorcrater/index.htm

Best Time to Visit: 10 a.m. to 5 p.m. Tuesdays through Saturdays, 1 p.m. to 5 p.m. Sundays.

Why Go: About 50,000 years ago, this big nickel-iron rock falls out of the sky and breaks up over West Texas, crashing at several locations and leaving behind a few meteor craters. But the Odessa area has lots of loose sand and high winds, so no one knew where they were. Then in the 1920s, folks nearby discovered the largest: about 550 feet in diameter and 100 feet deep. Today you can walk all around this National Natural Landmark. It'll take some imagination to visualize this jumble of rocks and sand as a meteor crater because it no longer has well-defined sides. But don't complain. Where else can you say you walked around a meteor crater? Once you complete the loop, turn around and go the other way because different

Odessa's Meteor Crater.
Photo by Allan C. Kimball

things are certain to catch your eye. The walk has several informational signs. A museum has recently been added where you can learn all about meteors and see a chunk of the one that caused this very crater.

Odessa—Presidential Museum

Length: Three quarters of a mile/easy
Location: Adjacent to the University of Texas-Permian Basin.
Information: 4919 E. University Blvd., Odessa, TX 79762, 432-363-7737, www.presidentialmuseum.org
Best Time to Visit: Hours 10 a.m. to 5 p.m. Tuesday through Saturday.
Why Go: Because two presidents, George H.W. Bush and George W. Bush, once called Odessa home, you might think this museum was built to honor them, but you'd be wrong. Back in 1964, the museum was established to honor recently assassinated President John F. Kennedy and expanded to include all of our nation's top executives. It now provides primary sources of information about the presidency for researchers. The rotunda of the museum features a huge replica of the carpet used by Kennedy when he occupied the Oval Office. Follow the exhibits

around the building to take in history and artifacts from each of the men who has occupied the office. One unusual touch is the dolls displaying replica ball gowns of each first lady. And because the Bushes did live here, they have a little extra: The modest home they used when George W. was an infant, authentically restored to a Christmas morning.

Odessa's Presidential Museum.
Photo by Allan C. Kimball

Panther Junction—Big Bend National Park

Trail: Lost Mine Peak
Length: 4.8 miles/strenuous
Location: The park's Visitors Center is 26 miles east of Study Butte at Panther Junction. Lost Mine Peak trailhead is along the Chisos Basin Road just before the road drops into the basin.

Information: P.O. Box 129, Big Bend National Park, TX 79834, 432-477-2251, www.nps.gov/bibe

Best Time to Visit: Anytime, but in summer start your walk in the morning as early as possible.

Why Go: This walk is much more of a hike than a walk, but it simply has to be included because it is one of the very best in Texas. And it's my favorite in the region. If you're physically able to do it, don't miss it. It's the most strenuous walk in this book because it begins at about a mile high and ascends for another 2,000 feet, but the trail is a good one and has a number of switchbacks, so you won't be exhausted when you reach the top. Getting to the top is part of the fun, because the trail takes you through two very different ecosystems as you gain elevation. But getting to the end of the trail is the supreme reward. You can relax on one of the rocks and gaze out over what seems to be the entire world below your feet. On a clear day, you can see for more than a hundred miles. If you get lucky, you might even spy an eagle soaring *below* you. The trail also has a self-guided brochure available at the trailhead to identify all the plants and trees you will pass along the way.

Lost Mine Peak Trail at Big Bend National Park. Photo by Madonna Kimball

Panther Junction—Big Bend National Park

Trail: Santa Elena Canyon

Length: 1.75 miles round trip/moderate

Location: At the end of the Ross Maxwell Scenic Drive.

Information: P.O. Box 129, Big Bend National Park, TX 79834, 432-477-2251, www.nps.gov/bibe

Best Time to Visit: Avoid summer afternoons when the return can be brutal.

Why Go: This is perhaps the most stunning canyon outside the Grand Canyon. It's not as long, deep, wide or even as geologically significant, but its sheer 1,500-foot-high cliffs are something to see from inside, at river level. The best way to experience the seven-mile-long canyon is on

Santa Elena Canyon at Big Bend National Park. Photo by Allan C. Kimball

a guided boat trip, but if you can't manage that, take this beautiful walk into its mouth. The trail begins where Terlingua Creek empties into the Rio Grande, then ascends several staircases on a cliff on the American side. A dirt trail then takes you up into the canyon—by riparian flora like huisache, river cane, tamarisk, and willow—until you can go no farther. If you spend any time in the canyon, you will marvel at the play of light and shadow as time changes the sight before you almost every moment. As you relax at the end of the trail in absolute serenity, you will be hard-pressed to remember this narrow stream is an international boundary and those cliffs on the other side are in a foreign country.

Panther Junction—Big Bend National Park

Trail: The Window

Length: 4 miles/easy down but strenuous on the return

Location: Trailhead near the park store in the Chisos Basin.

Information: P.O. Box 129, Big Bend National Park, TX 79834, 432-477-2251, www.nps.gov/bibe

Best Time to Visit: Avoid summer afternoons, when the return can be draining.

Why Go: This is a remarkable trail, completely delightful going down but a little strenuous on the return because it's uphill all the way. The Window is an unmistakable formation in the basin, a deep V illusion formed by two of the basin's cliffs. The trail is surrounded by the highest mountains in the park and at the beginning goes through an open plain, then along Oak Creek into a shady canyon to the end of the trail

The Window Trail at Big Bend National Park. Photo by Allan C. Kimball

where you discover a pour-off from the creek that drains most of the basin. Don't get too close to the edge; the rocks are slippery, and it's 200 feet down. Along the trail, you're likely to pass wildlife—foxes, javelinas, deer, even bears—especially if you go in the early morning. If you're feeling adventurous, take the quarter-mile Oak Spring Trail that veers off just before the Window. It will take you up to an amazing view of the desert below you. On the way back, you'll get panoramic views of the basin mountains, including Casa Grande. Make sure you take enough water in the warmer months.

Presidio—Big Bend Ranch State Park

Trail: Cinco Tinajas

Length: 1 mile round trip/easy

Location: 4 miles southeast of Presidio off Farm Road 170, then off Farm Road 169 (the Casa Piedra Road).

Information: P.O. Box 2319, Presidio, TX 79845, 432-358-4444, tpwd.texas.gov/state-parks/big-bend-ranch

Best Time to Visit: Avoid summers.

Why Go: No matter what you do in the heart of Big Bend Ranch State Park, it'll be a wild adventure. Just getting there is difficult: traveling 20 miles down a washboard dirt road to the park headquarters at La Sauceda, the old ranch house that is now a Visitors Center. You'll find the Cinco Tinajas trail along this road, about 1.5 miles west of La Sauceda. A tinaja is a hollow in the rocks that collects rainwater, a precious resource in the desert. This trail takes you down to a short slot canyon that is home to five of them, and you can see them from the head of the canyon or scramble up the cliff and see them from the rim. You can take a relatively easy walk up the west rim, or the most difficult one to the east rim—or do both to get the full impact of this very narrow canyon. Once up top, notice the awesome view of the empty desert all around you. You almost expect Clint Eastwood to come riding out of the haze accompanied by a Morricone Western film score. Nothing fits the Old West Texas stereotype more than Big Bend Ranch State Park.

Salt Flat—Guadalupe Mountains National Park

Trail: Devil's Hall

Length: 4.2-mile round trip/moderate

Location: The park is on U.S. 62, 35 miles southwest of White's City, N.M. Trailhead is in the Pine Springs Campground.

Information: 400 Pine Canyon Road, Salt Flat, TX 79847, 915-828-3251, www.nps.gov/gumo

Best Time to Visit: Anytime.

Why Go: Here's another walk that is more of a hike, but it's worthwhile. This is a classic example of the adage that the journey is more important than the destination. The destination here, Devil's Hall, is rather average considering other places in West Texas, but the trail is one of the great ones. Do not believe the park brochure that says this is a level trail—it's anything but. You will travel up and down, up and down, and up and down more times than you can count. Then you will scramble through a dry creek bed. And finally, near the end of the trail, you arrive at a truly unique feature: the Hiker's Staircase, a natural formation that looks exactly like some master stone mason cut steps into the rock face. Go on up to get to the end of the trail. Along the trail, you'll see maple trees and ponderosa pines, unusual flora in the Chihuahuan Desert.

Hiker's Staircase on the Devil's Hall Trail at Guadalupe Mountains National Park. Photo by George Colvin

Salt Flat—Guadalupe Mountains National Park

Trail: Mckittrick Canyon

Length: 4.8-mile round trip/moderate

Location: Trailhead is about 7 miles northeast of the Pine Springs Visitors Center.

Information: 400 Pine Canyon Road, Salt Flat, TX 79847, 915-828-3251, www.nps.gov/gumo

Best Time to Visit: Fall is best for leaf colors, but anytime is good.

Why Go: Another stroll that is more a hike than a walk, but certainly rewarding if the leaf colors are good in the fall. The blazing golds and reds of the maple trees in the canyon are not something you expect to discover in the middle of the desert. Go anytime, though, and you'll find a scenic canyon that contains a year-round spring-fed creek. Along the trail you'll wander through every ecosystem you can find in West Texas: desert, riparian, and woodlands. The diversity is amazing and the change from one to the other is subtle. You can also opt for the McKittrick Canyon Nature Trail that is only about a mile loop and is relatively easy. The trailhead is about 7 miles northeast of the Pine Springs Visitors Center.

San Angelo—River Walk

Trail: River Walk and Paseo de Santa Angela
Length: 4.75 miles/easy
Location: From 14th Street to Bell Street.
Information: San Angelo Chamber of Commerce, 418 West Ave. B, San Angelo, TX 76903, 325-655-4136, www.sanangelo.org/goodtimes/attractions.php
Best Time to Visit: Anytime, but summers can be very hot.
Why Go: Every city in Texas can learn something about how to create inviting, beautiful public spaces from San Angelo. None do it better. The River Walk is well-designed, beautifully landscaped, and for much of the distance has nice touches like pavers for the trail bed, sculptures here and there, public plazas, or the painted-on hopscotch board at Celebration Bridge. The walk is also adjacent to several city parks and goes by the impressive Visitors Center. Also be certain to take the Paseo de Santa Angela that passes by the Pearl of the Conchos mermaid statue in the Concho River and by the great new Fine Art Museum, by an old train depot, and end up at historic Fort Concho. Wandering through the museum and the fort, which you should, will add more mileage to your walk.

San Angelo's River Walk. Photo by Allan C. Kimball.

Terlingua—Ghost Town

Trail: Self-Guided Walking Tour

Length: 1.5 miles/easy

Location: In Terlingua Ghost Town along Farm Road 170, four miles west of Study Butte.

Information: Historic Terlingua, 100 Ivey St., P.O. Box 362, Terlingua, TX 79852, 432-371-2234, www.historic-terlingua.com.

Best Time to Visit: Anytime, dawn to dusk. Go early in the morning during the summer.

Why Go: The town, once a bustling community of 2,000 people digging cinnabar out of the ground to make mercury, was abandoned after World War II. The Chisos Mining Company was king then. Today, it's mostly a ghost town attracting tourists to its ruins, a great restaurant, and a top-rated gift shop. The walk will take you by many of the ruins, including stone or adobe *jacals* or huts that miners once lived in, a mine shaft, the crumbling mansion of the mine owner, a school, a church that is still in use, a jail, and a picturesque cemetery. The cemetery has more than 400 graves, some of them unmarked. Some of the more recent graves are decorated with plastic flowers or coins or beer cans—depending on the personality of the deceased.

*Perry Mansion ruins at Terlingua Ghost Town.
Photo by Allan C. Kimball.*

Pick up a brochure guide at the Terlingua Trading Company—and while there, roam this great shop for all sorts of goodies from Big Bend books to souvenirs to topographic maps. By the way, those locals sitting on the porch bench drinking beer are facing east to watch the sunset. Yes: east. Ask them.

For bulk sales and wholesale inquiries, contact:

Great Texas Line Press • Post Office Box 11105 • Fort Worth, Texas 76110
greattexas@hotmail.com • www.greattexasline.com • Tel. (800) 73TEXAS